Truth Is Symphonic

Hans Urs von Balthasar

Truth Is Symphonic

Aspects of Christian Pluralism

Translated by Graham Harrison

Ignatius Press San Francisco

Title of the German original:
Die Wahrheit ist symphonisch:
Aspekte des christlichen Pluralismus
© *1972 Johannes Verlag, Einsiedeln*

Cover by Victoria Hoke Lane

With ecclesiastical approval
© *1987 Ignatius Press, San Francisco*
All rights reserved
ISBN 0-89870-141-4
Library of Congress catalogue number 86-83131
Printed in the United States of America

Contents

Prologue. Truth Is Symphonic

I

Symphony means "sounding together". First there is sound, then different sounds and then we hear the different sounds singing together in a dance of sound. A bass trumpet is not the same as a piccolo; a cello is not a bassoon. The difference between the instruments must be as striking as possible. Each one keeps its utterly distinctive timbre, and the composer must write for each part in such a way that this timbre achieves its fullest effect. Bach is not the best example here, perhaps, adapting violin concertos for the harpsichord with only slight modification, but Mozart is the absolute master: his violin, horn or clarinet concertos always succeed in bringing out the pure essence of the instrument concerned. In the symphony, however, *all* the instruments are integrated in a whole sound. Mozart had this whole sound in his ear to such an extent that, on occasion, he could write down the single instrumental line of an entire movement because he "heard" it within the sym-phony of all the parts. The orchestra must be pluralist in order to unfold the wealth of the totality that resounds in the composer's mind.

The world is like a vast orchestra tuning up: each player plays to himself, while the audience take their seats and the conductor has not yet arrived. All the same, someone has struck an A on the piano, and a certain unity of atmosphere is established around it: they are tuning up for some common endeavor. Nor is the particular selection of instruments fortuitous: with their graded differences of qualities, they already form a kind of system of coordinates. The oboe, perhaps supported by the bassoon, will provide a foil to the corpus of strings, but could not do so effectively if the horns did not create a background linking the two sides of this counterpoint. The choice of instruments comes from the unity that, for the moment, lies silent in the open score on the conductor's podium—but soon, when the conductor taps with his baton, this unity will draw everything to itself and transport it, and then we shall see why each instrument is there.

In his revelation, God performs a symphony, and it is impossible to say which is richer: the seamless genius of his composition or the polyphonous orchestra of Creation that he has prepared to play it. Before the Word of God became man, the world orchestra was "fiddling" about without any plan: world views, religions, different concepts of the state, each one playing to itself. Somehow there is the feeling that this cacophonous jumble is only a "tuning up": the A can be heard through everything, like a kind of promise. "In many and various ways God spoke of old to our fathers by the prophets . . ." (Heb 1:1). Then came the Son, the "heir of all things", for whose sake the whole orchestra had been put together. As it performs God's symphony under the Son's direction, the meaning of its variety becomes clear.

8

The unity of the composition comes from God. That is why the world was, is and always will be pluralist (and—why not?—will be so increasingly). Of course, the world cannot get an overall view of its own pluralism, for the unity has never lain in the world either formerly or now. But the purpose of its pluralism is this: not to refuse to enter into the unity that lies in God and is imparted by him, but symphonically to get in tune with one another and give allegiance to the transcendent unity. As for the audience, none is envisaged other than the players themselves: by performing the divine symphony—the composition of which can in no way be deduced from the instruments, even in their totality—they discover why they have been assembled together. Initially, they stand or sit next to one another as strangers, in mutual contradiction, as it were. Suddenly, as the music begins, they realize how they are integrated. Not in unison, but what is far more beautiful—in sym-phony.

2

Today's situation, which must be our starting point, is characterized by an impatient tugging at the framework of a unity that is felt to be a prison. Isn't it unjust that a melody is trapped within a triple fugue, and that the law of the fugue governs how it shall develop—and even determines its original shape? The melody wants to escape from this conditional existence, developing and singing untrammeled.

Nowadays, there is a powerful urge to break through to the fascinating figure of Jesus Christ, to grasp him as he was, untrammeled, stripped of the damaging association with an institutional Church, a pile of unintelligible dogmas, obsolete customs and ossified traditions. He is to emerge from the detritus of two thousand years' history and stand before us in his original, simple, naked radiance. And at the very same time the science of exegesis is insisting that we can know about Jesus Christ only through the early Church's confessions of faith, that the accounts of his life are partially formed by this faith—that is, that we shall never be able to remove the ecclesiastical garments from him. Since this is irrefutable, a second struggle begins: the Church, with its two thousand years of growth, its wealth of tradition, is to be disrobed, purified, simplified until the (surmised) glory of Jesus Christ begins to shine through in it. This implies putting a question mark over even the earliest of the primitive Church's formulations of faith: are not they too a veil, an excrescence? Layer after layer of the onion is peeled away, and in the end the core is also gone.

But are not both attempts right, in some way? For surely the Church as a *totality* ought to be transparent, allowing Christ to shine through? Surely it should be nothing other than that? And if it no longer is, no wonder people try to get behind it to the essentials. On the other hand, if Jesus surrendered himself to death in order to make himself understood as a totality, from the yonder side of death, through his Resurrection and through appearing to his disciples and explaining himself to them, is it not clear that the Church is the place he himself has chosen, the place where he wishes to be present and accessible? What we call "God's Incarnation" in Jesus of Nazareth only comes to its fulfillment in the community of believers, who are aware of having been commissioned to announce this Incarnation to the world and to bear witness to it and represent it before the eyes of the world. And no one can say when the first community begins to be "incipiently Catholic". From the very beginning the structure of office is there, in Peter and extremely strongly in Paul; from the beginning Mary is there, praying in the midst of the community, the Mother who stood with John at the foot of the Cross. From the very beginning people are baptized; the bread is broken; sins are forgiven; the sick are healed; there are the laying on of hands, the issuing of detailed instructions, the institution of presbyters, the pronouncement of sacred judgments and the recourse to tradition. The various themes are already interrelated, attuned to each other; the fugue proceeds.

We cannot wrench Christ loose from the Church, nor can we dismantle the Church to get to Christ. If we really want to hear something intelligible, we are obliged to listen to the entire polyphony of revelation. We cannot make Christ shine through the Church by destroying it or replacing it with forms of community of our own designing. The only way is for Church people to model themselves as closely as possible on the reality of the Church—which is Christ's body and thus his bodily presence. On the other hand, it is utter folly to try to "grasp" Christ: he always slipped through the hands of those who wanted to seize him. He himself, in his entire reality, is only a transparency: "He who has seen me, has seen the Father"; "He who confesses the Son has the Father also"; "Do not hold me, for I have not yet ascended to the Father." We learn his secret by allowing him to return to his origin. And the Spirit who proceeds from Father and Son, since he is neither Father nor Son but their reciprocal love, introduces us into this mystery. Even eternal Truth itself is symphonic.

3

It is worth asking whether the Church was ever *less* pluralist than today, when there is so much talk of pluralism. The current slogans and manifestos, even if they are mutually contradictory, claim to be panaceas for a Church in crisis. Within the Church, people see all progress as coming from democratization and the involvement of everyone in decisions and from a corresponding "change in structures" that would really allow the democratic spirit to play an effective part. With regard to the Church's external relations, there is a similarly one-track demand for the Church to take sides on behalf of the poor and exploited with a degree of political commitment that does not even draw the line at revolution. Here, social and political action is the real service of worship and true prayer; it is also the thoroughgoing school of selflessness and renunciation.

These are strange curtailments of Christ's teaching and example, of the New Testament theology of the Church and, what is more, of the Vatican II program of "opening up to the world". For while such calls do draw attention to things that are necessary, they discriminate, with monotonous regularity, against things that are just as necessary from a Christian point of view. Is there no other way of exalting marriage but by devaluing celibacy for the sake of the Kingdom of Heaven? And if one wants to commend political action on the part of "the Church" (and such action can never be anything other than the action of particular members of the Church), is it necessary to say that the contemplative life of penance is useless and obsolete and to alienate it from the love of believers? And does the rediscovery of brotherly love as the central Christian commandment mean that interiority has become taboo, and that every direct relationship between man and God has to be dismissed as evasion or alienation? And when we exalt orthopraxy, right action, which is demanded clearly enough by Jesus himself ("he who does the will of my Father", Mt 7:21), do we have to lose all sense of what the New Testament equally emphatically calls right belief, orthodoxy ("anyone who . . . does not abide in the doctrine of Christ does not have God", 2 Jn 9)? The gospel of tolerance is preached with intolerance, the gospel of pluralism with a zeal that betrays its sectarian character by "tolerating" those who do not subscribe to it as old-fashioned and objects of pity.

What is going on? People cannot bear to have a unity that is above them and of which, with their particular tasks and graces, they are only a part. They shift unity from the whole into the part. They do not want symphony, but rather unison. In Platonic terms, this is the *tyrannis;* in modern terms it is totalitarianism, the inner contradiction of the one-party system and the arrogant claim to infallibility. These are the ideologies of one-dimensional man, who demands that everything fall within his worm's-eye view. Some people even try to draw up a blueprint for the present-day and future saint, forgetting that the first thing presupposed by sanctity is the will to be a part of the Body, with its many counterpoised members, and to perform the whole will of God wherever one is situated, one thus and another quite differently. No saint ever said that what he was doing was the *only* right thing. Mother Teresa is doing one thing in Calcutta; Abbé Monchanin has done something totally different in the same country. Both are proper manifestations of the "one thing necessary". All those who try to live by Christian love are on fire between God and the world, with God for the world representing the world for God, and the flame of their love always burns within the communion of the saints. They know that all ministries need each other. The priest in the world needs the Carmelite nun who prays and does penance for him in seclusion. He also needs the layman, who, with his own competence, puts into practice in the world the Christian attitude that the priest endeavors to mediate to him. The priest will not engage in political action himself, as if he were a layman, nor will the layman assume any role that belongs to the priestly office. "For the body does not consist of one member but of many. . . . If all were a single organ, where would the body be?" (1 Cor 12:14, 19).

Today, therefore, perhaps the most necessary thing to proclaim and take to heart is that Christian truth is symphonic. Sym-phony by no means implies a sickly sweet harmony lacking all tension. Great music is always dramatic: there is a continual process of intensification, followed by a release of tension at a higher level. But dissonance is not the same as cacophony. Nor is it the only way of maintaining the symphonic tension. Mozart imparts something winged, buoyant, internally vibrant to his simplest melody—how often he works with simple scales!—so that the power that enables us to recognize him after only a few bars seems to flow from an inexhaustible reservoir of blessed tension, filling and tautening every member.

The Church's reservoir, which lies at its core, is "the depth of the riches of God" in Jesus Christ. The Church exhibits this fullness in an inexhaustible multiplicity, which keeps flowing, irresistibly, from its unity.

In Part One of this book, we shall loosely assemble the various aspects of theological pluralism that are encountered as we circle around the heart of the Christian revelation. Part Two consists of examples that illustrate the way the multiplicity flows from the unity and is grounded and can at any time be reintegrated therein.

I. A tour through theological pluralism

a. Israel

Truth is not a thing, nor is it a system. It is One, or
rather, The One, possessing and determining itself in
its infinite freedom. It is genuinely self-determining
and thus holds together; it is not like a shapeless ocean,
flowing aimlessly and endlessly in all directions. When
the Old Testament says, "I am God, and also henceforth I am he; there is none who can deliver from my
hand; I work and who can hinder it?" (Is 43:13), we
sense the vigor of this self-determination in every
word. It would be ridiculous to think that a freedom of
this kind could be reduced to formulas and held fast
within them. We cannot even be sure that this God will
not suddenly decide, after decades or centuries, to
utter a further "Word of the Lord", announcing or
doing things that he alone can say and do, things that
no one could have imagined, no one could have deduced (for to do that, one would have to be like him).
Moreover, unique and unimaginable as such things
would be, man would still stand accused of culpable
neglect, for somehow there would be a familiar ring
about them, like the speech of man's childhood from
which he has become estranged. . . . The God who is
always making all things new is at the same time the
God of faithfulness, who remains *true to himself* and

thus also true to Israel. His freedom is not arbitrary action but truth; his rule is not the whim of the tyrant.

Thus, in the Old Covenant we find two spheres in an inseparable relationship, yet that never unite into a single orb. On the one hand is the sphere of the free and sovereign God, making himself known (by overpowering evidence) in his most manifold utterances as the sole, the living, the acting, the present One. On the other hand are the many instructions, interventions, punitive and forgiving judgments, reminders and past deeds and pronouncements, warnings against complacency and promises of things to come, that is, a complex of elements, not reducible to a system, constituting Israel's milieu, the milieu in which it is and can be (or could be) the "people of God". The Old Testament's structure of life and thought is in a true sense a complete pluralism, as such guaranteeing the complete unity and uniqueness of the sovereign God. Of course, there is no contradiction between the individual deeds and words of God—only the fool could imagine there were, albeit the wise are also liable to temptation in this matter—but God's dealings with David are unique. They cannot be deduced from his dealings with Hezekiah or Zedekiah or from his relationship with Moses. On the one side, there is a rich spectrum of colors, yet it is never so complete that pure white light could somehow be produced by intellectual manipulation. On the other side, there is the unapproachable furnace of light, discernible through all the refraction of colors, yet indicated by them only in an oblique and fragmentary way—no man, if he wants to remain alive, should desire to look directly at that furnace (Ex 33:20). It is in this many-hued reflection that Israel possesses the life of Yahweh, but it *really does possess it*. Indeed, Israel is ceaselessly plagued with experiences that, frequently enough, it would rather be without. Such experiences demonstrate unmistakably to Israel that its faith in God is no illusion, that it has not fallen for some ideological superstructure. The pluralism of revelations was irreducible, and the center whence they clearly sprang was sovereignly free and thus could not be deduced. These were the simultaneous and disconcerting facts that Israel had to swallow; this was the school it had to go through so that it should become clear who this God is who deigns to render himself understandable to men. Only on the basis of this insight could a path be forged to the ultimate plan of God in his self-revelation, namely, Incarnation.

b. God and his Word

God's words do not come to us like arrows in an ambush; they do not strike us without our knowing who shot them. Every god who speaks to men surrenders something of himself in doing so, for there is no language common to the multiplicity of gods. Each god only speaks his own language, utters himself and in speaking gives away his own, unmistakable name. That is why, among primitive peoples, there is the almost inseparable association between the name of the god and magic. When a god speaks, one somehow learns his name. He has surrendered his essential secret and man has power over him. Let us not smile at the simplicity of primitive peoples, for it would be only too easy for anyone to show that Christians too have attempted this kind of magic: armed with God's own revealed secret, they have advanced toward him to unmask and overpower him with their theological rationalism and idealism, until in the end he dies the death of atheism. Such could be the history of Christian and post-Christian modern times.

Moses too asks God what his name is. It sounds naive to us, or at least like something of another time. Can the One who "is all"—not, however, as the sum total of his works but as he who is "greater than all his works" (Sir 43:28)—be designated by a name in the way determinate things are identified by genera and species? Is he not of necessity the One named in all names, which means that no name can embrace him? And yet, when he speaks, his words are determinate and intelligible, implying that he is also determinate, and since he is God he is not determined by any other but by himself. That is his freedom: not some general freedom he shares with other things, but his exclusive freedom. His freedom, his self-determination, his name: they are one and the same. When God speaks to Moses, his word—with its determinate character—has the unmistakable sound of his freedom. That is how it is recognized: he and no other! It is quite clear who is speaking. And to that extent (and to that extent alone) the name of God is revealed in his word. What God entrusts to Moses, so that he may proclaim it to the people, is both things: a "name", meaning that he will be in constant touch with his people, he will be present with them and accompany them with his efficient word—and also an assurance that this accompanying One (however his name may be formulated) is the same God who was with the patriarchs. It is a new development, yet it contains an element of "what was from the beginning". The response on the part of the people corresponds to this: it must be open to receive the word anew each time, and at the same time it has a security that reaches back to the beginning. But this security is only given on the basis of a receptivity that must be continually renewed.

This is the most difficult lesson Israel has to learn: it must be purely receptive toward him who determines—because in himself he is the perfectly, ineffably freely determined One—and who gives himself in this determinate word of his. He reveals himself totally, holding nothing back, yet in such a way that no one can lay hold of him. Anyone who tries to do that is no longer a recipient and thus grasps a mere nothing—empty words. So, cannot God be taken at his Word, cannot he be committed? Only in the way he gives himself and has always given himself: he has to be received; he cannot be ensnared. We can remind God of his great deeds in the past and of his promises that point to the future. We are justified in doing this, provided we take this broad spectrum of time into the narrow, acute place where we decide to be recipients, that is, dedicate ourselves to a constantly renewed obedience. We cannot put our trust in God for tomorrow on the basis of what happened yesterday if today, when we approach him, we are doubting, faithless and disobedient.

The same applies to the breadth of God's word as an

utterance concerning himself. In the course of time such words are multiplied. People experience many things about God. He is mighty, righteous, merciful. He issues particular, very precise demands. He keeps his promises, but visits the iniquity of the fathers upon the children to the fourth generation. He punishes Israel's enemies and also uses them to punish Israel. He puts his word into the mouths of particular men. These bearers of his word have a mysterious influence with God: they can plead for God's saving help; they can call down disaster. . . . All this and many other things are known about God. A pluralism of statements and propositions comes into being; people acquire knowledge in terms of history, prophesy and law. But the strange thing is that all this knowledge tells us far less *what* God is than *who* he is. It has to come to a halt in face of the freedom of his revelation. (The so-called Nominalists were onto something here, but they were not able to express it properly.) This freedom often looks like arbitrary whim *(potentia absoluta)*. God can be wrathful, and the next moment, at a word from Moses, he can be pacified. He can announce the ruin of Nineveh, and then, to the prophet's annoyance, he can forgive the city, since it has repented. He can anoint a king and then reject him for what seems to be some small thing. Such action is not arbitrary, however: it is simply absolute sovereign freedom, which never contradicts itself—as Paul shows in connection with the rejection of Israel for the sake of God's having mercy on the Gentiles (Rom 11:29). But it is impossible to say in advance how, in each case, God's paradoxical dealings actually comprehend and confirm his abiding "attributes", his truth, goodness, righteousness, faithfulness and mercy. The various propositions cannot be set in order. The totally unperturbed way his word disseminates a pluralism of initially irreconcilable statements about his dealings with men (and hence about himself) testifies to his tremendous, sovereign, absolute self-determination. To accuse him of contradicting himself would be a contradiction on our part. Man is always trying to assemble the multifarious aspects of truth under a single principle that he can grasp. But if the freedom of the God who speaks (and this freedom is also his truth and faithfulness) is evidently the sole principle by which we can understand these words and give them meaning, we must give up the idea of possessing this principle ourselves. All man can do is continually receive it, and since the principle concerned is God himself in his self-determination, it is to him that man must refer the plurality-in-unity of faith, obedience and understanding.

Faith exhibits a reticence, a renunciation that holds back and allows the God who speaks to take the initiative. It is only by thus making room for the plurality of the word that the believer acquires a faculty for discerning the meaning of the particular words uttered by the speaker. And insofar as the speaker wishes to communicate himself, this meaning is none other than he. This is the all-embracing, all-pervading meaning of the individual words, imparting meaning to everything—and we always presuppose that God's words are effective and creative. For this free self-communication we have the word *love*. It is therefore the sole hermeneutical principle for understanding the Bible. If it is lost or supplanted by another, we are bound to lose our way in a welter of particular interpretations, and only the personal principle can be our Ariadne's thread to lead us through. Israel was well aware of this when it formulated as the chief commandment man's total response to God's revelation (understood as "love")— "with all your heart, with all your soul and with all your might"—indicating, with beautiful and reverent indirectness, that this total response was naturally intended only as an echo of the meaning of God's word, that is, the totality of all his words.

Thus, resulting from the initiative of God himself, we have the explicit manifestation of something that shines through all religious phenomena the world over, once they are liberated from the darkness of demonic fear and the equally demonic urge to manipulate—not primarily a need (to worship something, to abase oneself before it), but the awareness of having received something, which calls for a spiritual "making room", quiescence, listening, faith, so that understanding may take place. There must be a renunciation of understanding as something I possess in order that the Whole, whose approach and nearness are sensed, may interpret itself. Among peoples why do not hear or hardly hear the particular word made known to Israel, various techniques of listening in silence take its place. They are not totally astray, yet they yield no ultimate success. There may be a pluralism of techniques, but they all converge on one transcendental act that almost universally prescribes or intends a state of openness and readiness. Since here the Absolute does not speak with the same definiteness as that found in

Israel, there is a far less clear awareness that the plurality of world phenomena is positively fraught with the self-communication of the Absolute. In differing degrees, the plural aspect of the world is regarded as lacking being and is thus excluded from essential religious experience. Israel, by contrast, is at least on the way toward interpreting the cosmic hieroglyphs, on the basis of the verbal revelation, as utterances of God. But only when, in Jesus Christ, God himself mastered the speech of human existence, did it become possible—beyond all expectation—for human existence to be read in the same way. The problems of pluralism are taken over from the Old Covenant into the New, where they become in many respects more acute.

c. Jesus Christ, the Word of God

Jesus Christ is this free, sovereignly acting and proclaiming Word of God in the form of a human life, which is characterized by birth and death, joy and pain, family ties and personal relationships. The focus of free and inaccessible light penetrates this human being without ceasing to be what it necessarily is: "Glory in the highest". But ultimately it reveals itself as what it always was: "goodness and loving-kindness" (Titus 3:4) and even "gentleness and lowliness of heart" (Mt 11:29).

Now everything becomes infinitely more complex, precisely because it seems to have become more tightly interwoven. Indeed, it is so complex that a human being might despair of understanding and formulating

27

any of it, if it were not for Jesus' "Fear not, it is I", and his encouraging "Thou hast hidden these things from the wise and understanding and revealed them to babes" (Mt 11:25).

Now we hear from the mouth of Jesus Christ the authoritative "But I say unto you . . .", which the prophets had proclaimed as the Word of Yahweh in former times, and his human "I" thus acquires an inconceivable intensity and awesome majesty, for it will decide the eternal destiny of whoever encounters him and indeed of all men. The "I" of Jesus Christ is the measure of God's distance from and nearness to man, that unimaginable nearness of him who is, and remains, even more unimaginably sublime above everything in the world *(in similitudine major dissimilitudo)*—and both things are equally true. We shall never be in a position to encapsulate the mystery of this "I", with its nearness and its distance, in a concept or a formula, for at its heart lies the mystery of the relationship between God, the Absolute, and man, the relative. But if the deeds and words of God radiate from this focus in Jesus Christ, does not this mean that they can be referred to the center found in his "I", as the spectrum of light is traced to its source? And does not this result, after all, in a kind of overall order (in the way what a man says can be seen to be in accord with his character traits) and hence a kind of "system"?

Yes and No. Yes, because God really wishes to be seen and heard and touched in his incarnate Word of life so that we, responding to his approach, may enter an entirely new fellowship with him. We are not meant to linger on the fringes, fascinated by fragmentary prismatic colors, but to advance from all directions toward the heart of that central light that has come near to us. No, because he who approaches us from this center is not just any man: in this fellowman we encounter the eternal God, and he is so near to us that now his nearness is far more mysterious than his former sublime distance. All his utterances have a Christ quality, which, far more than in the Old Testament, reveals their plurality as aspects of unity.[1] It is he who shines forth in them all, and so all features exhibit a greater kindred relationship with each other, an *air de famille,* common to even the greatest opposites, such as sovereignty and the attitude of the servant, power and defenselessness, Cross and Resurrection. And once more No, because precisely this drawing closer of the source of light and the spectrum of colors at the periphery renders the Whole less accessible to an overall view. Why? Because what we have, in terms of the

[1] So it is not because the plurality of Old Testament theologies migrates over into the New Testament that the latter contains a plurality of approaches toward a theology that can never be fitted into a unitary scheme. The plurality that characterizes the preliminary nature of the Old Testament (which has not yet attained its unity in Christ) is transcended in the sovereign unity which is Christ and which the Holy Spirit interprets in this multiplicity of approaches. It is rather that, in a totally new and unforseeable way, the new unity, which is a present unity, *freely plays with* the plurality it has assimilated and made into its expressive body. If it wishes to, it can allow the Old Testament motifs an almost independent sphere of play (e.g., the prophecies of a future world transformation) and then go on to show that their content is fulfilled to overflowing in its own unity (of life-death-resurrection).

deeds and words of Jesus, exhibits a far clearer profile than one would expect from almost random emanations, as it were, of his infinitely richer personal life, a life with the Father, in the Holy Spirit, for his fellowmen and for the life of the world.

Under the Old Covenant, in times when the prophetic word was silent, there was the temptation to arrange God's commands as a Torah, making a kind of system and "law" out of them, although the best Israelites were always aware that there was something presumptuous about this. Faced with Jesus Christ, however, it would be utterly fantastic to attempt such a thing. Separating his deeds and words from his spontaneous and sovereign person would be in flagrant contradiction with these same deeds and words: they are "spirit and life", written not on stone or parchment but in "fleshy tables of the heart" (2 Cor 3:3). If there is still to be a Holy Writ to bear witness to the words and deeds of Jesus, it must continually point away from the letter and the system and toward what is embodied, by God's Spirit, in Jesus Christ. Insofar as he is a real embodiment ("the Word became flesh"), the danger of materializing, as a result of the desire for system and for intellectual manipulation, is greater than in the Old Testament. But insofar as Jesus Christ, the ever-flowing source, dwelt among us and remains with us through the outpouring of his Holy Spirit, this urge to manipulate is continually broken up by the superabundance of freedom and vitality that cannot be contained in any vessel. The oil of the widow of Sarepta will never fail anymore, even if there are no jars in which to put it.

d. The interpersonal Thou: an image and an approach

The fact that in Jesus Christ we encounter a fellow human being and an interpersonal Thou (and also the divine Thou) provides us with a way into the mystery; it puts into our hands the most important thread to guide us through the labyrinth. No one would dream of arranging the lifetime's utterances of another man—as in a biography, for instance—into a "system". All the same, interpreted with insight, they can all draw attention to his characteristic vitality and spontaneity; they can teach us to understand and love him. Even if we are dealing with him every day, another man remains a more or less open secret—but a secret all the same. Of course, we are familiar with a whole range of naturally given situations, gestures and reactions that we understand on the basis of our common humanity and shared customs according to rules of thumb. But within and beyond this there is always a personal sphere, which while it expresses itself in and through the commonly understood is by no means reducible to it. The stronger and more original a personality is, the more its utterances spring from its own unique and as such inaccessible interiority, which reveals its richness precisely by the wealth and unpredictability of its manifestations. All human relationships are characterized by elements of self-revelation within a context of mystery. This is what makes them valuable and thrilling—which applies to the most intimate exchanges in sexual intercourse, too, if it is the expression of genuine personal love. Communicating the incommunicable: this paradox is nowhere more evident than here. Nor is it a tragic mystery, either: it is a mystery full of bliss and promise. My partner must be allowed room in which to reveal himself freely, as both "I" and "Thou", so that he can give himself and be accepted by me.

In its dialectic between "grasping" and "letting be", and as the ability to interpret something that, of its own volition, breaks into my whole spiritual sphere from beyond it, the understanding of another human being always surpasses the "categorical" and the "transcendental". There is no "category" in the "I" for this particular, free "Thou"; it cannot be subsumed under any other heading. All I can do is be open to it and wait and see how it will enter its unique message into my "system of categories". On this view, the realm of human relationships no doubt constitutes the privileged place where we can grasp what is meant by divine revelation in Jesus Christ.

Naturally, there is also a danger here, and for two reasons. In the first place, the human "I" of Jesus Christ extends (in a way that is beyond our comprehension) into the being and the speech of a divine "I", which means that it is not altogether proper to apply our accustomed interpretation of natural human acts and gestures to this particular fellowman. For God does not share a common nature with us. If his sovereign freedom makes use, in Jesus Christ, of our nature in order to approach us and render himself intelligible to us, even the purely natural acts of Jesus Christ are to be interpreted in the unique, divine context of his freedom. Everything about him bespeaks divine initiative, a spontaneous movement toward us that cannot be traced to any other cause—at a deeper level, everything natural about him is grace. To the God who speaks, the humanity of Jesus is what is spoken to the one who speaks. The difficulty is that we cannot exclusively allot the free, speaking "I" of Jesus to either of the two spheres. That is the mystery of Christology—reflection upon it was bound to lead to formulations such as those of the first Councils. It is customary to say that everything in Jesus Christ is wholly human and wholly divine. That is true, but we must remember that between the human and the divine there is the distance of ever greater dissimilitude. Distance is not the same thing as an alienating gulf. If a word of Jesus seemed close to us, familiar, while at the same time we were afraid that its divine meaning remained alien and unintelligible, Jesus would not be the Word and the revelation of God. When he weeps over Jerusalem, we understand, from a human point of view, the human sorrow he expresses. But in faith, we also understand that God, in his eternal mystery, could not have found a clearer way of expressing his attitude to the Jerusalem of the day than in these tears of unrequited love. He weeps these tears so that we may grow nearer to the heart of God. The more unreserved the human heart is in preparing itself in faith and love to receive the revelation of the divine mystery, the more lastingly it will be penetrated and taken possession of by the actual divine meaning. The insight that comes by faith has countless degrees, but this does not mean that the mystery can be erected stage by stage on these steps and changed into concepts emptied of mystery. Our very relationships with our fellowmen will preserve us from this illusion. We can get to know the intimate side of a fellow human being. Such knowledge introduces us more deeply to his freedom (that cannot be manipulated), and in fact, instead of diminishing this freedom grows with our knowledge of it, and we grow into it.

e. Truth as body

Jesus Christ described himself as "the truth", a word that cannot be de-fined (de-limited) because it refers to something in-finite; it can only be approached asymptotically by countless definitions. He is truth insofar as he is the ultimate higher integration of all God's individual self-revelations down through history: all of them are centered on his "I". Whatever truth is, it is judged, aligned and instituted from this center. His "I" is the organic and organizing focus of truth. The theology of the schools put it in this way: the God revealed in Jesus Christ is theology's formal object. There are two conclusions to be drawn from this.

First, if the truth that Christ is and represents has a number (in fact, an infinite number) of individual aspects, they are all related to his center as are members to the totality of the living body. And there can only be a living body if it is animated and governed from the center of a soul that expresses itself as "I". The living body is truly remarkable. It can be regarded and treated from outside as an object—but as far as the "I" possessing it is concerned, it is by no means as objective as the rest of the exterior world. It is "part of me": it is the way I am present to the world. I feel my body

34

from inside, and this feeling is immediate to me and an essential part of my normal consciousness. On the one hand, the Letter to the Colossians says, "the whole fullness of deity dwells bodily" in Christ (2:9); on the other hand, Ephesians says that the Church is the body of Christ, "the fullness of him who fills all in all" (1:23). Thus, everything we could become aware of in terms of objectified knowledge of God is concentrated in Christ's subject; in his subjectivity Christ lives out the truth of God so that we may apprehend it. The whole organism of the Church in all its parts, that is, preaching, the sacraments, the conduct of Christian existence, those "truths of faith" that are put forward to be believed more or less explicitly as dogma—all this is only objectified when seen from without. From within, these things are in reality modes of existence of Christ, who is at work in the world through his living Holy Spirit. He alone can measure exactly the meaning and scope of each of these features. For instance, when holy Scripture seems to present itself as the objective spoken word of God, we must never forget that at the same time it is always the "speaking word", which Origen calls "the one body of truth" (Comm. Jn 13, 46) or "the perfect body of the *Logos*" (Jer. hom. 39, fragment) or "the one perfect instrument of God" (Comm. Mt. 2, fragment). Thus, what from the outside looks like the letter is from the inside the Spirit, who blows where he will. The letters are innumerable; the more creativity the Spirit displays in expressing himself, the less they can be matched with him. Scripture witnesses that the letter cannot keep pace with the fullness of Christ in its attempt to express it: if everything that Jesus actually did were to be written down, "I suppose that the world itself could not contain the books that would be written" (Jn 21:25). Without destroying the fundamental norm given in the Bible and the Church's dogma, the living speech of the God who reveals himself is able continually to create new organs of life and utterance as the history of the Church unfolds; they share in the truth to the extent that they purely express God's activity and speech. The more full of energy the self-expressing unity is, the more it can present itself in multifarious and even unexpected and highly imaginative ways.

This brings us to our second conclusion. The principle of unity, which alone enables us to set the pluralist utterances in order, and hence to understand them, is not itself objectified in such a way that the uttering (subject) becomes the uttered (object). It can never be manipulated by man, by the theologian, for example, in an attempt to build a system of divine truth or of absolute knowledge from it. It remains the "I" of God in Christ, which can never be given to us in such a way that it eventually ceases to be given. So, too, it can never be received in such a way that the act of reception—faith, worship, love, thanksgiving—is something lying behind us in the past. The Christian, in his acting and thinking, the theologian, in his task of trying to establish the pattern—each of them knows, of course, where the center of the pattern is that will enable him to relate the plurality of elements, but access to this center is granted him only in the act whereby Christ freely embraces him in grace. And this act can never be formulated. Where the formula, in its fixed abstractness, makes clear its relation to the concrete, free fullness of Christ, there is hope that theological insight may take place. For as we know, this fullness wishes to (and takes steps to) communicate itself in all its modes of expression. But we have yet to see how the fullness can yield a practically applicable criterion for the right path to knowledge.

f. The heightened paradox

First, we must go once again beyond the level we have reached so far. We have seen that man is open to other men in a way that transcends categories—thus he can receive, understand and respond to the self-expression of another's freedom. This openness was the precondition of his receptivity for the infinitely more free self-revelation of the one God, who cannot be understood in terms of genera and species. This God, who is infinite self-determination, certainly has the power to render himself intelligible as he desires to each of his creatures; in his purpose of self-expression he cannot be the victim of the creature's tragic failure to understand. How could the One who created language not be in a position to speak and be understood? All the same, the creature, when spoken to, is always aware of God's divinity and hence that God is beyond his grasp (for this grasp goes no further than a mere intimation that all things have an inaccessible origin and end—which leaves us cold). Thus we are aware of a mystery that concerns us infinitely. Our creatureliness itself must be inchoately aware that the ultimate horizon of our existence is beyond our grasp, that is, there must be an embryonic "religious sense" at a deeper level, which can be awakened—otherwise the mystery that comes near to us in revelation would never make any impression on us. But more important than this inchoate awareness is the world's mystery that the God-who-comes opens up to us.

How and why can this paradox be heightened? Is it enough to say that the sinner who turns away from God loses interest in him (or even loses the faculty for apprehending him), and that God is now speaking to closed ears and consequently has to employ new and stronger means to make himself understood? No, it is not enough, although there is some truth in it: the incarnation of God in Jesus Christ does have this aspect of being a really tangible means, a way of addressing the hard of hearing. The deeper significance is this: in this altered and adapted language God himself actually takes on the deafness of his hearers, and no longer as a tactical or purely pedagogical move but as an act of that love that seeks to fashion itself after the beloved. Now the final word is not revelation and precept but participation, *communio*. And that in turn, beyond word and deed, implies suffering. It means occupying the place of total and universal closedness, that is, God-forsakenness. God's Word in Jesus Christ wishes to die with us in this God-forsakenness and descend with us into eternal banishment from God.

Luther's dictum, that at this point revelation *"latet sub contrario"* (lies hidden in its opposite), is not too strong, provided it means no more than it formally says. Jesus is in fact the Lord who empties himself, taking the form of a slave. He is the Son, defined by his ultimate intimacy with the Father, but he dies in complete estrangement. He is the sign of God's presence in the world, but in death he cries God's absence so stridently that the darkened world trembles and the curtain veiling sacred things is torn, exposing naked profanity. And God takes this Word, which had descended into the ultimate silence of spiritual death, and brings him back to himself in Christ's resurrection; this Word, speaking hiddenly and in the form of its opposite, he sets forth and proclaims to the world as his pristine and complete truth.

We must note, however, that in the formula *latet sub contrario* both aspects (the attribute and its opposite, the proposition and what contradicts it) have the same subject. The identity of this subject, namely, God in the man Jesus Christ, is not threatened by these contrary aspects. According to Philippians, the same person appears now in the form of God, now in the form of a slave, and in the Gospel this same subject can say, "The hour is coming . . . when you will leave me alone; yet I am not alone, for the Father is with me" (Jn 16:32), and a little later, "My God, my God, why hast thou forsaken me?" (Mk 15:34). The experiences of the same subject are in contradictory modes, but they do not assail his identity. Prior to the Cross, Jesus can know that even in the coming experience of forsakenness he will not be forsaken by the Father; on the Cross itself, he experiences this forsakenness so deeply, for the sake of sinners, that he no longer feels or knows anything of the Father's presence. His relationship with the Father is indestructible; he says, "My God"—but this God is hidden *sub contrario*. Indeed, the very profundity of his forsakenness is the sign of him who so profoundly conceals himself. Since the subject, God's Son—in this case identical with his abiding connaturality with the Father-God—holds on so tenaciously through the contrary modes of experience, it is superfluous to go against all the evidence of the text and ascribe particular attributes of his first state (that is, the beatific vision of the Father) to him in his second state. His forsakenness affects his entire relationship with the Father; the mists envelop even the mountain peaks—but, walking through the valley of darkness, it does not cease being what it is, namely, sheer dependence, absolute obedience on the basis of boundless love.

This ability to be itself *sub contrario* is originally the prerogative of the all-powerful divine love, of God in his absolute freedom who actually can determine "not to spare" his only Son but "to give him for the life of the world" (which is in darkness). It is very precisely the manifestation of the almighty power of the Only God, who shares his glory (and here it is!) with no one. It is the prerogative of God's only Son, who, as his Word, thus demonstrates God's truthfulness to the uttermost. The divine truth is rendered neither demonic nor inaccessible by this means, nor, by taking the godlessness of the emancipated world on himself, does God become subject to an extrinsic law of destiny that would thereby reveal itself as the real, governing law of the world, the "law of dialectic". All the same, since it is a question of encompassing the world in all its profanity—for its relation to God has been profaned—

there can be no stopping halfway once the path of "concealment in the opposite" has been taken up. It must be followed to the very end: "He descended into hell."

g. The organs of truth in the heightened paradox

If this is the case, then all the organs or gestures of the divine Word in the world must necessarily share in this communion on the part of God with the sinful world, must share in this process of dying and descending into the concealing opposite and rising again on the far side. For if Jesus is *the* Son and *the* Word of the Father, and as such takes on himself the adventure of such a total dying, the *Logos* of God (and hence theological logic itself) is involved in a movement in which nothing that belongs to the *Logos*—and first and foremost the Church, with all its forms of expression—can remain untouched. So it would be wrong to think that the Church had some kind of immortal framework exempt from destiny (often referred to nowadays pejoratively as "institution") that, while it is inhabited and represented by vulnerable human beings with their changing roles, is somehow timeless. Just as there is nothing abstract about the principle embodied in Christ, everything being incarnated in a unique and personal way, there is nothing abstract about the Church principle. It is not abstracted from human beings of flesh and blood but exists in them, subject as they are to the law of death and resurrection. The official side of the Church shares the fate of the apostle:

41

if he meets with sneering, denial, scorn and crucifixion, it will too. The official side of the Church, mortal as it is, triumphs as a spiritual power that is strong when it is weak. "I die every day"; "we are always being given up to death." This applies to Paul *to the extent that* he is a bearer of office, "and behold, we live", "so that the life of Jesus may be manifested in our mortal flesh". What applies to office in the Church also applies to the sacraments, to preaching and to theology. It applies to the Bible just as much as to the Church's tradition.

I do not wish to be misunderstood here.[2] In his experience of being forsaken by God, Jesus Christ was not handed over to sin, to demons. Humanly speaking, he is never more closely and more anxiously followed by the Father. For it is in the most complete

[2] I have already been misunderstood here. The chapter "Papst heute" in *Klarstellungen* (1971) ["The Pope today" in *Elucidations* (SPCK, 1975)] was crudely misunderstood—as an attack on the hierarchy—by Dr. J. P. Michael in the *Anzeiger für die katholische Geistlichkeit* and Prof. A. Schenker in *Neues Volk*. It is very strange that I should have been credited with such an attack. But it shows the baneful influence of the view that it is not the structures of the Church which share in the destiny of Christ, but, at the most, those persons who happen to be the Church's representatives. This prejudice comes from a sociological mode of thought that sees the Church along the lines of a purely human institution and forgets that everything in it is "the fullness of Christ", however much it simultaneously has its worldly and (all too) human side. We can only repeat what was said in *Elucidations:* the suffering, the humiliation on the part of hierarchical office (humiliation even at the very heart of the Church) is a sign that the Lord is with his (official) Church; it is even a means used by God to render this office more credible in its discipleship of the Lord, so that he can be seen through it.

obedience that he pursues his path into complete darkness. This path is the unswerving institution of the divine redemption of the world, which no demon can approach. No false step is possible in this divine darkness. Where the Son feels himself weakest, he is strongest: the Church Fathers, mystics and theologians have turned their attention to this paradox thousands of times. Outwardly it may seem that men cause Christ's Passion: they put him in chains, scourge and crucify him; they pierce his heart. But inwardly it is a trinitarian action, in which God has the chief role and men are merely supernumeraries.

It is somewhat analogous to the organs of Christ's fullness in the world. They are oppressed, threatened and put to death by human beings (both inside and outside the Church), but at a deeper level they are guided by God himself along the Christ's "royal path", where no gates of hell are able to overcome them. "A servant is not greater than his master. If they persecuted me, they will persecute you" (Jn 15:20), but "not a hair is to perish from the head of any of you" (Acts 27:34). The Church Fathers, led by Origen, compared the Church to the moon *(pulchra ut luna),* in part because, like the latter, it receives all light from the sun (Christ) and then is nearest to the sun when, as the new moon, it has disappeared, that is, when it shares most intimately in Christ's mystery of suffering.

h. *Paradox and pluralism*

However, there seems to be a great danger in this participation of Christ's organs in his heightened paradox, in that all the forms of secular truth (real or illusory) met with along this path of destiny thereby receive some share in the truth of Christ. If he has borne the fate of the godless in all its forms, every form of this fate must indicate a phase of his journey. In that case, we are faced with a limitless pluralism, which even has the benefit of strict theological and christological support.[3] If the opposing points of view are fitted into a thoroughgoing system, as in Hegel's dialectic, none of them, however peculiar and eccentric, can drop out of the system of truth. In fact, this yields an inner relatedness of the Absolute, the One, to all its possible prismatic refractions, which can be reintegrated into the fullness of concrete unity in "absolute knowledge".

What has happened here is that the standpoint of God, who freely discloses himself to the world, has been equated with the standpoint of man, who has adopted God's revelation as a universal law of being and now imagines that he can use it as a key to all mysteries. Furthermore, man has identified the law of God's revelation *sub contrario* to the closed world, that is, the law of God's most incomprehensible love, which descends into the depths with sinners, with this universal law of being. In doing so he has banished from it the dimension of freedom, the *gratis* aspect of unmanipulable grace. His soul is lost; all that remains is a clattering mechanism. The One, self-determining

---

[3] Cf., e.g., G.Morel S.J., *Nietzsche,* 3 vols, (Paris: Aubier, 1971). For a criticism cf. G. Chantraine, "Rationalité théologique et décision" in *Seminarium* 2 (1971): 240–66.

God no longer has the freedom to give his revelation in the world that contingent particularity that distinguishes it from the other features of the world and points to his free, loving act. This determinate particularity is submerged in the endless plethora of world features, which ultimately, in their random plurality, can all be read as revelations of the self-interpreting One.

That would be to remove God's absolute, personal point of reference in the world, the event of Jesus Christ, from its privileged position. The fact that he puts himself *sub contrario* in his enemy's place, in solidarity with him, is no longer the highest and freest expression of his ever-constant love (which never turns into its opposite), which becomes undialectically graspable to the believer, but the expression of a law of occurrence whose functioning can be manipulated and monitored. World events are no longer judged and ordered according to his inalienable freedom. He himself is bound by the overall law of dialectic: it is the latter that dictates his place in the cosmos of forms.

We are faced, therefore, with two totally different pluralisms, which diverge at their outset and develop along mutually irreconcilable lines. In the first, we have the "ever-greater dissimilarity" between the free God and free man (the *analogia entis*), in which God has an unrivaled primacy. In the second, the law of dialectic (which arises from a secularized Christology of which man has taken charge) embraces God and the world, and the One and the many become two sides of the same Being (pure logic with the inner motion of dialectics). True, if the event of the Cross really is the

ultimate, free expression of the whole relationship between the guilty world and God reconciling himself
with it, his language cannot be totally foreign to the
world: the world languages (as forms expressing
human existence) must be constituted in such a way
that they can be assimilated into this ultimate, all-
comprehending Word, not as if a universal dialectical
law (of a "speculative Good Friday") were to subsume
the Cross of Christ to itself. In the structure of the
world and of existence, therefore, there must be a kind
of adumbration, a sketch, an inchoate intimation of the
Cross, a preliminary plan on God's part that is aware of
the imminent culpability of the free human being and
takes account of it, without man being able to guess it,
abstract it as a universal law and gain control of it.[4]
The plan can be carried out exclusively by the almighty power of God, who can lead Christ down to
hell only because he is powerful enough to bring him
up again (Dt 32:39; 1 Sam 2:6; Tob 13:2; Wis 16:13).
There is no such thing as a speculative resurrection
from the dead: there can only be a real one.

It is clear now that it is not every *Weltanschauung* or
philosophy that can provide the foundation for rational
reflection on divine revelation (of the Old and New
Covenants). Rather it is God, in his freedom to determine himself and his revelation, who, in the act of
revelation itself, judges between the philosophies. A
philosophy can only be used as a vehicle for the (decidedly indispensable) preunderstanding of revelation

[4] Cf. A. von Speyr, *Schöpfung* (Einsiedeln: Johannes Verlag,
1972).

provided it is already open, or can be made open by theology, to the primacy of God's sovereign freedom. In revelation itself, man is challenged to acquire a particular view of existence.

i. The pluralism of world views

Let us dwell a little on this topic, for since the beginning of Christianity it has been a constant preoccupation, and today's problem of pluralism is ultimately only a new variant.

If we begin with the ancient world, we must be careful not to let our remoteness from it, which causes the mountain profiles to merge into one another, deceive us with regard to the brokenness of its spiritual landscape. Like India, for example, Hellas presents us with diametrically opposed and irreconcilable world views. Materialisms and hedonisms jostle with idealisms and ethics of duty, radical individualisms contradict the predominant collectivisms, and theistic doctrines of the ground of the world are disputed by sceptical and atheistic views. And if, in later ages, these elements are cast into the melting pot, what emerge are not forms having a certain internal unity but, for the most part, only hybrid chimeras, which only a real thinker (like Plotinus) is able to refashion into a substantial entity. The most diverse theories are on the market, and most buyers are not particularly selective: they take a little of all of them.

There is a lot of decadence here, but behind the decay it is clear that even the apparent thoroughbred forms are by no means spontaneous phenomena. All the great philosophies come into being through dialogue and disagreement with one another. Whether they agree or disagree, continue a line of thought or achieve a synthesis of various predecessors, they all have an osmotic effect on each other. Plato presupposes both Parmenides and Heraclitus, and Aristotle (to say nothing of the Stoa) is unthinkable apart from Plato. Plotinus' concluding synthesis succeeds in fusing Aristotelian and Stoic elements in an original form of Platonism. This early round-table discussion of the great philosophies has nothing to do with eclecticism—a term that should only be applied to syntheses that have been insufficiently thought through. It is humanity, thinking symphonically, polyphonically. And it is characteristic of its greatest thinkers that the intuitions at the heart of their systems always assimilate scattered elements they find to hand. So it is with great art as well: it is always indebted to its antecedents, putting the final stone in place at last where many before had attempted to build. Thomas Aquinas is perhaps the most extreme example: his originality lies, not exclusively but substantially, in his lucid arrangement of the vast and confused volume of thought that had preceded him.

In mentioning Thomas, we have touched on the topic of philosophical "transposition". An entire *Weltanschauung* can be transposed from its native key into another without suffering any harm. Did Thomas transpose the world view of Augustine and Dionysius into that of Aristotle, or vice versa? Or did he translate both of them into a new, third modality? Endless questions arise at this point, which would provide discussion material for the schools for centuries, and the Platonic and Augustinian purists will never agree with the Thomist purists. It would be best not to debate the theories but the issue itself, which concerned all the great architects of the spirit without exception. Fichte and the other idealists transposed Kant. But Marx, too, made a transposition of Hegel, and it was Marechal's view—in his transposition between Thomas and Kant—that, using care, the methods of both men were reversible. There has never been a single philosophy, not even in the case of Hegel (for Marx has unmistakable objections to him). There is only philosophizing humanity, ceaselessly circling in dialogue around the riddle of the being of the world, and life, and man, and history and death.

But this dialogue does contain, after all, elements held in common. We find this dualism throughout. On the one hand, there is the principle through which the world comes about and through which people attempt to think about the world; on the other hand, there is the plenitude of things and consequences that follow from this principle. But is the principle the world itself, or is it above and prior to the world? Is it matter or spirit? Conscious or unconscious? The twilight quality of existence, exhibiting many aspects, many ways into the mystery, may cause one or the other hypothesis to seem more probable. Yet it is certain that the principle, the originating ground, is different in nature from the phenomenal world. But how different? Here we come up against contrary longings in man: ultimately, perhaps, he may want to hold onto the best in life, life's "idea", and take it with him into an eternal life. Or perhaps he wishes for a radical and conclusive end to all that leaves him unsatisfied and the thirst for transitory things. Or perhaps he would want his limited consciousness (which is like a prison) to open up at last to the dimensions of the world (and thus dissolve as an individual consciousness); but since the world itself is finite and transparent, consciousness would have to expand even further, to the limitlessness of the Ultimate Ground itself. . . . And then, if all these longings were to be fulfilled, the Ultimate Ground would have to be both: the unitary epitome, the "idea" of the world—and at the same time, going beyond it, the Wholly Other.

The philosophies move within the horizon of questions such as these; the purpose of their debate is primarily to prevent the glowing fire of the question being extinguished. This can happen in two ways. On the one hand, there is resignation (giving up the question); on the other hand, there is the assertion that the question has been answered and has thus vanished. The first, resignation, is a tremendous impoverishment of the human being, who, tired of asking questions, deliberately limits himself to a circumscribed foreground area, settles down individually and socially in his small world and, with the help of organization and technology, endeavors to make life as bearable as possible for himself and those who come after him. But since he has deliberately cut the umbilical cord binding him to the world's ground, he lacks all orientation to the Absolute and goes round in circles within relative values, which, of course, mutually threaten and destroy each other. Resignation cannot be kept to the periphery; it pervades everything and gives it a stale taste. At this point, the second form of non-philosophy takes over, that is, the affirmation that there is no substantial question beyond what is generally knowable, or at least none for which solutions can be found, as in the case of secular programs. Such a statement only holds up if the person making it identifies himself with the principle or Ultimate Ground itself. Everything is given in and for the sake of consciousness, and if (in evolution) consciousness comes at the end, it is because it has provided its own preconditions. Put differently: everything that is not consciousness is an alienated form of consciousness and, by effort, can be transformed back into its proper mode—the world of man for man. These willful ways of denying the question take their revenge by turning into their opposite, namely, the total devaluing of the concrete that had been made so absolute. Thus extreme left-Hegelian-Marxist ideologies become almost interchangeable with Buddhist approaches. For within the world views of the ancient world too there lurks the temptation to seize the underlying principle: Atman is equated with Brahman, or (in Plato) souls are said to be as eternal as God, or (in the Stoa) the spark of the individual soul is held to spring from the divine fire at the center and eventually to return thither.

It was necessary to give this doubtless popularizing and dilettante outline of what is known as *Weltanschauung* or philosophy in order to gain a grip on the problem of the encounter of revelation and philosophical pluralism. Philosophy, radically conceived (and not

in the grotesque manifestations of its decay), can really
be nothing other than *philo-sophia*: a love that yearns
for wisdom. Neither philistine resignation nor the titanesque, arrogant attempt to seize absolute wisdom is
philosophy. Revelation can come to terms with every
form of the genuine philosophy that seeks to plumb
the difference between the world's ground and existence, whether such philosophy comes from the Medi-
terranean world, the Far East or Africa. But the dialogue will begin by eliciting the question that is
fundamental to philosophy and is contained in and
behind the various answers that are apt to conceal the
question. Paul does this in Athens, for instance, by
drawing attention to the inscription "to the [or to an]
unknown God" behind all the "known" gods, proclaiming to the philosophers "what you worship as
unknown". He describes this original Ground as the
source of "life, breath and everything" and acknowledges that there is a relationship between creature and
Creator, as the poets had said: "For we are indeed his
offspring" (Acts 17:23ff.). A few hundred years later,
Paul would have been able to put the emphasis more
on the "greater dissimilarity" of negative theology. If
he had been dealing with Buddhists, he would have
affirmed the abiding "unknown" quality of the God
who reveals himself in Christ, and who becomes more
mysterious the nearer he approaches us. From the
same perspective, he would have been able to discuss
the theme of the unity of Atman and Brahman, provided that the Unknown is and remains himself and
cannot be dethroned by any techniques of spiritual
self-exaltation or self-absorption.

The plurality of genuine philosophy arises from the plurality of aspects of earthly existence and also, as we have seen, from man's partially contradictory longings with regard to his ultimate destiny. Does he really want to be immortal? As an individual or only as a tribe or a genus? Is it presumption vis-à-vis the Infinite to cherish such wishes? Is it not more pious to surrender one's "I" in God? Is not this "I" an illusion, a prison, into which some prenatal guilt has locked us? When revelation engages in dialogue with the seeking human being, it leaves him with all his—often contradictory—approaches; it does not compel him to follow a single path of thought that alone brings salvation. It also leaves him with his contradictory feelings; to their confused tangle it only offers its simple message: God loves the world; he loves you personally and has demonstrated it in Jesus Christ. In saying this, it has uttered what is decisive, even if these words have infinite implications that the hearer will realize at an appropriate time. Then, too, it will emerge that the plurality of tentative human endeavors and of real or supposed needs actually converge on the truth of this statement, without being able to anticipate it in the slightest.

Revelation thus uncovers the inchoate and essentially incomplete character of philosophies and world views. Again, Paul puts this with perfect precision in his Areopagus address: God has placed men on the earth "that they should seek God, in the hope that they might grope after him and find him. Yet he is not far from each one of us . . ." (Acts 17:27). This search is guided by the knowledge of a presence, and not only some vague, general presence, but a presence that is personal to each individual; the search, though it naturally wants to "find", has no immanent guarantee that it *will* find ("in the hope that they *might* . . ."), for it is up to God and his freedom if and when he will be found. Great philosophies or religious world views have an intimation of the inchoate character of all attempts to get beyond the intramundane sciences *(meta ta physika),* which is why they are open to each other and ultimately speak in myths (Plato) or admit that they cannot be brought to a conclusion (as Aristotle said, "We must continue to inquire further and further into what Being is"). It is understandable that they all succumb more or less to the temptation to put a fixed or temporary roof on their edifice; it is human, it is above all part of "Original Sin", insofar as this phrase expresses mankind's titanesque urge to gain control of the world formula, to gain likeness to Zeus through stealing fire.

So revelation has no choice but to remove this roof superstructure and dismantle the philosophies until it uncovers the genuine search common to them all. The search will be expressed in a plurality of approaches; what unites them is the "restless heart". But as for the fundamentally proud and complacent systems that vaunt themselves as coherent systems of absolute truth, it must demolish them—*deposuit potentes de sede*—perhaps utilizing individual elements in a totally new context. Once admitted, the poverty of the question (which is nothing to be ashamed of, but is in fact the nobility of the creature in its naked exposure to the mystery) results in the appropriate language, in which God, who wishes to show us the rich poverty of his love, can speak to us *(et exaltavit humiles).* And since it is only God's free self-disclosure that can produce the key to the riddle of why there is a world at all; why sin, suffering and death are allowed in it; and what, in his futile existence, the creature may hope for, all philosophies whatsoever will need a transvaluation of their fundamental position. It is hard to say which of them, after such transposition, will be better adapted to serve as a spiritual vehicle for revelation and which will be less suitable. The thought of India, for instance, will have to accept much correction at a deep level, namely, that the world is a positive factor, freely envisaged by the Absolute, and that suffering too, since it has been taken up by the divine love, has a positive value; that earthly action and initiative on behalf of one's fellowmen is meaningful and compatible with contemplation. If these correctives can be assimilated, the original Indian sense of "God" (or the Absolute) would be closer to that of the Old and New Testaments than the world view of Western cultures.

There is therefore no cause for dismay in the idea that the truth of revelation, which was originally cast in Hellenistic concepts by the great Councils, could equally be recast in Indian or Chinese concepts. The Greek concepts themselves had to be widened in a way that came close to a new coining (for example, *hypostasis*) in order to be made at all suitable for the new content. Nor would the Indian and Chinese concepts be able to avoid a similar transmutation.

However, revelation cannot be translated into the subphilosophical theorems that, like particular disciplines, accept unquestioned axioms (for example, the existence of matter or of life or of society) and yet act as if they were quasi-philosophical elucidations of the total horizon. In this linguistic context, revelation has nothing to say, since no question arises to which it alone can give an answer. First of all, it would be necessary to overcome the refusal to face the crucial question—for example, the torturing riddle of individual death that contradicts personal love[5]—if this framework of thought and language were to be made capable of a dialogue with revelation. Or rather—since such attitudes are far too convinced of their own rightness to regard their refusal as a defect—man would first of all have to be freed from this constraining web, so that eventually a genuine question could grow within him, to which the Word of God could give an answer.

This is particularly the case today, when for the most part it is these subphilosophical theorems that are being taken as the basis of a qualitatively new and unrestricted theological pluralism. What I have in mind here are only the limited and often mutually exclusive horizons of the particular disciplines (for example, mathematical logic, linguistic analysis, psychology, sociology, physics), each of which tends to make totalitarian claims to explain existence. It is important for Christians to engage in these sciences not simply because of their countless positive, theoretical and practical results, but also in order to uncover their intrinsic limitations and incompetence when it comes

[5] Gabriel Marcel has dealt authoritatively with this topic.

to asking fundamental questions of *Weltanschauung,* on which the meaning or meaninglessness of existence ultimately depends, and to which only God's revelation in Christ can vouchsafe an answer.

j. *The Word of God in human speech*

The first question is not, "How can we human beings translate the one revelation of God into our many languages and thought forms?" The first question is asked by God himself: "How shall I cause my unique and utterly determinate Word to enter into the plurality of human languages and thought forms?"

We have seen that language (as the expression of thought) is a human phenomenon. And just as humanity, in all its variety, is one (thus any man can beget children of any woman), the multiplicity of human language is a many-branched but coherent organism. The languages and forms of thought familiar to us are the results of cross-fertilization, in part identifiable and in part lost in the oblivion of prehistory. It is an obscurantist abstraction to regard them as monads.

When God wishes to express his unique message in human language, he has to make do with the whole network of the world's thought forms and modes of speech. This is no disadvantage for him, however, for the divine Word he has to utter is much richer than can be plumbed by all of mankind's languages and thought forms taken together. In the event of Pentecost God symbolically expresses the fact that his first concern and prerogative are to utter his determinate and unique message with equal clarity in all human languages. (Earlier theology did not tire of interpreting Pentecost as the prototype of Catholic and genuinely universal pluralism; this has almost been forgotten nowadays, when people imagine they have discovered pluralism for the first time.) At the beginning of the Church's history, the miracle of Pentecost proclaims both the will and the power of the divine Spirit to make himself universally understood, with a clearly defined and in no way vague message in the greatest diversity of world languages. In this context we can pass over the question as to how the miracle took place (in those who spoke or in those who heard—in earlier times there was much discussion of this point), and indeed whether it took place in this concrete form at all or if it was rather Luke's comprehensive image for what happened during the first mission. However this may be, it is quite clear what the depiction means. Also, as tradition continually pointed out, the aim was to present a positive counterstroke to the Tower of Babel's confusion of languages. If human hubris planned to construct a unity that would reach to the divine, and this very thing resulted in men failing to understand each other anymore (for no one understood God anymore either), now God himself, having "learned" from the Cross of Christ from within how to understand us, will be able to speak to us all in such a way that we shall understand him and understand each other in him and in his language. Thus, as people listen to Peter's preaching, a dialogue arises of itself: "How is it that we hear, each of us in his own native language? . . . We hear them telling in our own tongues the mighty works of God." Now they all understand these mighty deeds and begin talking about them.

So God is not committed to Hebrew, or to Greek or to Latin. God's language is first and foremost his own: the event of his incarnate Word, Jesus Christ. God speaks in his flesh; he speaks in what Jesus Christ is and does and suffers. He speaks in the works of Jesus, and also, certainly, in the words of Jesus, but the latter's words are only a limited part of the Word that he is. It is a part that must always be seen in the context of all the rest, that is, his work, his suffering and in particular his being. "I am the life, the Resurrection, the door, the truth, the way": these are not actually sayings, but rather pointers to the uniqueness of his being, amplifications of his "*But I* (say unto you . . .)". These words would be meaningless, fantastic nonsense if it were not he who utters them. And if he had not suffered "for us", as the primitive Church says, his words would be presumptuous, suspect, lacking warranty. The Whole is a single Word; it extends its meaning in multifarious ways yet always holds it together. Consequently, it does not matter to us a great deal how many of the words go back to Jesus himself and how many to the Holy Spirit, who, according to Jesus' promise, will continue to interpret him in human languages and concepts. The kernel, the grain of wheat appointed to grow, is the irreducibly given, the absolutely unexplainable, which alone imparts meaning and context to the whole development—namely, that a man, an indubitably genuine and authentic human being, comes onto the stage claiming to represent God. He is different from him in that he calls him

Father and the One who sent him, and yet there is an identity too, since every man's relationship to God is determined by his relationship to this man Jesus. This kernel is so paradoxical that we can discern in it the whole incomprehensibility of God coming near to us.

This being so, it is no wonder that we already find a plurality of "Christologies" in the New Testament. If it were otherwise, the incomprehensibility of God, whose Word became flesh, would be at an end. The various promises and foreshadowings[6] stream from afar, from the Old Covenant, in concentric circles, each scarcely to be harmonized with the others. Thus in earthly terms, no one can be both sacrificing priest *and* sacrificed lamb, both the one humiliated to death for the sake of the people *and* the second prophet and leader announced by Moses; nor can we envisage how someone can fill the law to the last iota *and* at the same time free people from the yoke of the law "which neither our fathers nor we have been able to bear". Theologies that seem contradictory converge in a synthesis that surpasses them all in the fulfillment found in Jesus. Radiating from him, therefore, and ceaselessly circling around his mystery, paths lead off in all directions. In the Gospels, we can discern a gradual broadening and rounding out of the perspectives, but we must never forget that Paul (around 40 A.D.) had already discovered all the essentials: that Jesus was the Son of God, that the Cross and Resurrection were "for us" and even Christ's preexistence, however this may be understood. As in a kind of spontaneous genera-

---

[6] Cf. *Herrlichkeit* vol. III 2/2 Alter Bund (1967): 371ff.

tion, "the" dogma is already there from the outset, read off from the conduct and destiny of Jesus, subsequently to be unfolded in New Testament and later Church theology. This means that it is unjustified to assume that a Christology concentrating on the *event* of the Servant's exaltation to the Lord (Acts 2:36) is more primitive than one that stresses the *condition* of the Lord as servant (Mt 23:8ff.) or one based on the brief reflection that no one can be "exalted" to *divine* dignity unless, in whatever mysterious way, he already possesses this divine dignity. Thus, the christological problem is referred back to a theological one, namely, how motion can coexist with rest, becoming with being in God.

In the hiatus between the mortal "Jesus of history" and the risen Lord "who dies no more"—a hiatus bridged by the identity of the bodily person of Jesus— many different Christologies can arise. But if they are to remain really Christ-ologies they must all take their stand within the all-embracing mystery. In the attempt to take the humanity of Jesus totally seriously, one could take his (humanly necessarily) limited and time-bound horizon of thought as the starting point and have him expect an imminent end of the world, as did his apocalyptically minded contemporaries. But what if this horizon of thought were in his case a function of a unique sense of mission, which convinced him that, through his own destiny, he was to arrive at the *real* end of the world in a totally different and unique way, which he actually did?[7] Again, what if this undoubt-

[7] Cf. "Glaube und Naherwartung" in *Zuerst Gottes Reich* (Benziger, 1966)

edly inerrant consciousness of mission were accompanied by a genuine "not knowing the hour", because, in fulfilling his task, pure obedience was more important than the possession of a knowledge that would have limited the purity of this obedience as expressing the purest relationship with God? Hence the knowledge was determined and limited by the obedience. Patristic *kyrios*-Christologies all had considerable difficulty in conceiving this limitation and making it credible because, while they glimpsed the law of the *sub contrario,* it had not been followed through in all its consequences. So the real temptation in the first centuries was the tendency to Monophysitism. This, while it rightly emphasized that everything human in Christ allowed the divinity to shine through, constructed a rigid image of the divine as an eternally unmoved substance that was prohibited from expressing itself seriously *sub contrario* in finitude, obedience, suffering and death. Indeed, how the two things are related, the sublimity in the humility—this is a mystery that, in its uniqueness, cannot be fitted into any system. It can only be anticipated in some way by the various Christologies.

Similarly unapproachable is the mystery of the "for us", which was first discerned in apostolic times. We undervalue its realism if we only speak of the infinite worth of Christ's suffering or of his total guiltlessness, so that these two taken together result in a surplus of merit that can be applied to all sinners. But as soon as we try to go further and envisage a real inclusion of all the sufferings due to sinners in the one suffering of Jesus (which from an earthly point of view is decidedly limited), we seem to get into realms of myth and fantasy. Should we therefore shift the center of gravity from the Cross to God's antecedent desire for reconciliation, which reveals itself, in the powerful and effectual symbol of the Cross of Christ, as ever present through all time? Here we would be falling back into a kind of soteriological Monophysitism—which is fashionable nowadays—undermining Jesus' solidarity with us that is founded on his suffering and hence too our mutual solidarity in him. This would be to empty out the mystery of the communion of saints, whereby we can do things for and on behalf of one another, which is often described as the most profound of the Catholic mysteries. Up to now the convergence of the pluralism of Christologies has achieved little with regard to this central point. Particularly as behind the problem of the real (and not merely symbolic) representation[8] there is the deeper one of the freedom retained by the sinner (or actually restored to him), whereby he can acknowledge what has been done for him and his eternal salvation or reject it. Does this mean that man can wreck the entire salvific enterprise of God (who, after all, has shared in carrying his grievous sin, his hardness of heart) by extricating himself from the all-embracing *communio* founded by God and thus ultimately triumphing over God (in hell)?

Before criticizing the Christologies for their inability to offer more than pluralist approximations, it is salutary to realize what terrifying questions they are faced with. All these questions are addressed to God

[8] *Stellvertretung:* Christ's "standing in our place" [Tr.].

himself and concern his being and activity; thus it would be strange indeed if the human being got any further than wondering how God, in Jesus Christ, could possibly want to offer us love in such prodigality.

k. The criterion of dogma

This conclusion unexpectedly provides us with a criterion of the highest universality and adequacy by which we can judge the permissible limits of a theological pluralism. So far we have only discussed it with reference to certain aspects of Christology; we could just as properly have illustrated it by the doctrines of the Trinity and the Church, which are both inseparable from Christology. The issue is the same in all three areas—God in himself, God coming to us, God among us—namely, "the Father loves you" (Jn 16:27). This is expressed with all possible definiteness by the Word of God, which shows itself in Jesus Christ to be *the* Son of the Father. To say that God loves us would be an empty phrase—looking at the world as it is—had it not been substantiated by the Incarnation, Cross and Resurrection of Jesus, by his absolute solidarity with us, and had it not involved a revelation of the innermost nature of God (Trinity as love) through Jesus' relationship with the Father in the Holy Spirit.

This is the "matter" to which every dogmatic and theological formula refers, since every Christian act of faith embraces, not the formula or theorem, but the *res,* the "matter" referred to: *"Actus credentis non termi-*

natur ad enuntiabile, sed ad rem" (Thomas, *Summa,* II-II q
1, a 1 ad 1). But if, in order to encounter the *res,*
expression is necessary, in which expressions is encounter possible, and in which not?

For the encounter to take place, the expression must
cause the act of God's love for us to appear more
divine, more radical, more complete and at the same
time more unimaginable and improbable. The criterion is that of *maximality,* which succeeds (in a way that
is beyond our grasp) in incorporating aspects that
human reason would like to regard as incompatible
with the *res.* In fact, we can say this: wherever, in our
elucidation of the mystery, some aspect appears really
lucidly clear from a rational point of view, causing the
mystery quality (which announces the "greater dissimilarity" of God, his distinctive divinity) to retreat at
that point and opening up a wider spiritual landscape—there heresy is to be found, or at least the
boundary of permissible theological pluralism has
been overstepped. For when this happens, the *intellec-
tus fidei* has been eclipsed, and only human reason is
operating; instead of man's total act, responding in
faith to the ever-greater, incomprehensible love of
God, we have an act that has rationally domesticated
this love, at least in part. This almost always involves
taking one of two or more apparently contradictory
statements of the word of God and making it absolute,
and then this isolated proposition (which is an *enuntiabile* and not the *res*) is used as the basis for further
logical deduction.

A classical example of this is the doctrine of double
predestination (irrespective of whether *ante* or *post*

praevisa merita). According to this, God's sublime fore-knowledge has from the outset appointed a number of men to eternal bliss and a number to eternal damnation. People can adduce God's absolute sovereignty in support of this, but also man's freedom. They can quote passages such as Matthew 25. They can do all this without noticing that they have clearly moved away from the central message of revelation and, having reduced the mystery of God's dealings with us to a logic, they have robbed him of his divinity. Does this mean that we are forced to adopt the converse teaching of the "restoration of all things" and the abolition of hell? By no means. For that too would be to rationalize the love that is only encountered where it actually takes place, a love that demands our participation. We cannot man an observation post over and against this love. The Christian hope for the world is something quite different from rational *reportage*.

Our theme is the maximality of God's love, but as it encounters us in Jesus Christ, that is, in a divinely willed poverty and humiliation. Man cannot throw this love back in heaven's face with the excuse that he had a different idea of God's sublimity. We are presented with the image of the child (and it is more than an image): this is how the Kingdom of God is to be accepted. It is indeed a matter of acceptance, of God's coming to us and living in us, which requires more of us than a mere belief in propositions. In Jesus' life, death and Resurrection "for us" God has actually entered into the center of our nature and personhood, but it is in the outpouring of the divine Spirit into our hearts that this objectively given reality comes alive, subjectively, "for us" and "for God" in us. And once again it is impossible to subject everything to objective reflection in a way that will satisfy the reason. The child does not reflect on how and why it is loved or on what it must do to return love. Certainly, within the mystery that has come to us and penetrates us, there is the quite definite "command" to "abide" in the love of Jesus, and as we participate in this love and proceed from initial experience to deeper experience, there are norms and laws that can be formulated. But in each case, they always draw their rationale and credibility from the mystery of love given and received. And the more deeply a person realizes this gift and lives by it, the more he will see how little he matches up to it. The saint is right, contrary to all those who see him from the outside, to feel that he is the worst sinner and failure. Here we see quite clearly that the total acceptance of the gift of God's love in unreflecting child-likeness is the very opposite of magic. Magic is an enterprise issuing from human power that, at most, would seek to hold the divine fast *before* us (if such a thing were possible); it could never admit the divine *into* us. In the language of *eros,* it is the total abandon in which the bride allows the bridegroom to penetrate her intimately. The complete and yet simple faith that Jesus requires guarantees the success of that reciprocity of love that is God's aim.

It is only in this context that we can properly understand what "dogma" is, namely, a proposition that, whether it is positive (affirming things against rational negations) or negative (distinguishing itself from false positions), says that God's love extends to this maximum. Every dogma contains within itself the one, entire mystery. And insofar as the mystery is always the same, whole and entire, we can say that there is only one dogma (that the God who is love is there for us). But insofar as the mystery is inexhaustible in its fullness, in its aspects and consequences, the one dogma can be unfolded into a countless number of propositions. It is not the details of this development that are important, but the few great signposts that either give a warning—do not be deflected here, or the mystery will disappear—or encouragement—do not hesitate here, for God's love goes further. It also brings together things that appear irreconcilable. For instance, God is so free that he can actually carry out his creature's will ("merit", "intercession", "cooperation") *provided* the creature has allowed himself to be initiated inwardly into the mind of God. God can be so really present in his Church that it can act with his full authority ("office"), because on the other hand it has so perfectly received the Spirit ("Mary") that it can make an adequate response to him ("Thy will be done on earth as it is in heaven"). And this applies irrespective of all the grumblers who object that the empirical Church looks very different. Dogma, in being reflected back from the figure of Jesus Christ, can and must shed light on the conditions that make his appearance possible and on the origin of the mystery in God. It can and must illuminate the ineradicable difference between the One who sends, the One who is sent and that Spirit who is promised at the moment the Son returns to the Father. We shall have to speak very quietly and not stray so much as a foot's breadth away from the phenomenon of Christ, or we shall succumb to *speculatio majestatis*. Yet something must be said to preserve the mystery of "God is Love" intact: he is not love simply because he loves us (as if we are necessary to him so that he can be love); he is love in himself, he is unimaginable, eternal self-giving and self-exchanging. "Dogma" is understood by the simple because they sense the mystery in the words and take the words as pointing to it.

At this point we should once more reflect on what we have already said about truth as body and organs of divine life, but now under the aspect of the maximality criterion. Christianity is the embodying of God in all earnest. This earnestness is not some enthusiastic dream to the effect that the totality of the cosmos has now become God's body, or even that cosmic evolution signifies God's progressive embodying and becoming concrete. Christ was one among millions, and the Cross and Resurrection of the One took place on behalf of these millions. There is nothing quantitative about the presence of the Absolute and Perfect: it is the qualitative vindication of a perfect loving obedience.

Part of this vindication is "the body of Christ, which is the Church": visible, composed of distinct members as was his physical body. From outside it resembles a human association, with its entrance qualifications and other regulations. From within it is his real presence in the Eucharist, and the whole organism is permeated with his Spirit. Here again we need to apply the maximality criterion in dealing with the concrete form of this presence (in the various Christian denominations).

Furthermore, it calls for a maximum of unity in the body of Christ that is the Church, together with a maximum of diversity of members. According to Paul, the existence at the same time of the richest pluralism of Christian and ecclesial missions and tasks and of the complete unanimity of these disparate functions in love is the mark of the one body. It is the unity of love that calls for pluriformity, produces it and holds it together within itself. Without it there would be no living body but only sheer disparity. The privilege of my having a unique, personal form does not come from my empty freedom but from the unity that puts forth its multifarious members. *"Accedat, credat, incorporetur, ut vivificetur; non abhorreat a compagine membrorum"* (Augustine, *In Ioan.* 26). We receive our distinctness when we are ready and open for the Whole. This original unity determines the Church's concrete shape: it is not we who unite to build the Church; we "come to that living stone . . . and like living stones are ourselves built into a spiritual house" (1 Pet 2:4f.). The sacramental frame guarantees that we *receive* prior to being able to give a response and prior to being told what our role is. And, lest this priority of being receivers should be reserved for charismatics, the Church is from the very outset supplied with office, ministry (as witnessed by unequivocal texts), which has the role of summoning and assembling believers together as "Church", and of taking the initiative in making God's Word and his here-and-now sacramental deeds available to the community in a living way. This office is pure service, as Jesus hammered home to his disciples—and the fact that those performing this service are to take the lowest place, as Paul says, clearly shows that it has to do with Cross and humiliation and as such is essentially a form of Christ's presence. It continually reminds us that, as "the Son can do nothing of his own accord, but only what he sees the Father doing" (Jn 5:19), the Christian can only develop his freedom of action within an area that always comes to him as gift and in a highly concrete form, namely, the area of the complete freedom of God.

In this area, the Christian is called to participate in the work of Christ and to "complete" it—although in itself it is already finished. We have to endure this tension: Christ did not fall from heaven like a meteor and create a *fait accompli;* he was our fellowman and, while his work was admittedly totally unlike any other, all-embracing and on behalf of all, he could only perform it (and only wished to perform it) together with his fellowmen. It is true, of course, to say that we want to love and obey him out of gratitude for all that he has given us. But it is not enough. God's work, carried out in Christ, is to be continued in history and so is incarnated in our efforts, however much we may be aware of our shortcomings and are far from comparing ourselves with Christ.

Since we are "maximalists", however, we have confidence that the divine love is powerful enough to ensure that the Church exists prior to the believer, not only in terms of (Petrine) office, as objective holiness, but also as the perfect (Marian) response and correspondence. In this way it can provide a basis for Christ being really "with us"—for otherwise, from an earthly point of view, no fellowship would be possible with people such as us, prone as we are to fail and to misunderstand—as well as implanting into the Church a principle of subjective holiness that cherishes our faltering consent in a maternal way and causes the "ideal" (eschatological) Church to be really incarnated at a central point. Churches that lack these two principles (which fundamentally belong together as external and internal unity) will always manifest a certain abstract, nonincarnate aspect, constantly in danger either of dissolving into the purely pneumatic, which has no solid structure or stability, or of understanding themselves in purely sociological terms, which does not do justice to the presence of the living Christ organizing his body.

This is a highly compressed (and thus easily misunderstood) summary of the way in which the criterion of maximality can be applied to distinguish what is Christian. As we see in Christ, the maximal is always necessarily the most exposed and most vulnerable; also, where sinful men are involved, it is the most easily abused. The law of the *sub contrario* operating in Christ meant that he was bound to be a rock of offense, a stone of stumbling. The true Church is equally bound to bear this mark, and in a twofold way: on the one hand, it is rightly a scandal to the world because of the way it is abused by Christians, and on the other hand, above and beyond this, it will always remain a scandal per se in virtue of its christological and incarnate form.

Thus, whereas in the former case it is the Church's fault that many cannot or will not identify themselves with it at all (or do so only partially), in the latter case it must nonetheless continue to call people in the name of Christ to be totally identified with it in its incarnational form. And it is the difference between these two aspects that challenges the Church to be continually reforming itself.

1. Partial and total identification

A large number of Christians today can only partially identify themselves with the Church as it is manifested in history. They measure it against an ideal picture they have and find it substantially deficient. It may be that they measure it against a picture of Jesus they imagine they can draw, and perhaps find it totally superfluous or warped by contrast; for them, the Church is the disappointing ersatz that appeared when the Kingdom of God failed to arrive. This partial identification marks our period more profoundly than formerly, for numerous reasons. There is the inability to see beyond sociological externals and get to the central significance of Church structure; there is the view that, like other social forms, the Church can be evaluated according to its temporal efficiency. And above all there is the inability—not only on the part of outsiders or ordinary believers but also of the clergy and theologians—to see the organic unity of fundamental dogmatic propositions, to see that the individual items are interwoven and mutually confirm and strengthen each other. As a result, they are left with a brute juxtaposition of "truths of faith", some of which are evident and some of which are not, and from which they can choose what suits them. Consequently, there arises an inordinate number of constellations, a pluralism of selections made on the basis of consciously subjective perspectives, to challenge the whole edifice that is maintained and defended by an apparently dwindling number of faithful champions—who are labelled "integralists" on account of their fanatical holding fast to the entirety of the Church's system.

In our very first sentence we observed that God's truth, which resounds throughout the world through Christ and, in him, through the Church, cannot be a system. For God is not a system, and no system can represent God. Nor, in retrospect, on the basis of a revelation that has actually taken place, can we calculate the conditions that made it possible by taking what we know of God's maximal love and deducing what it must imply for itself and for the world. Paul's dictum still applies: "Know the love of Christ which surpasses knowledge, that you may be filled with all the fullness of God" (Eph 3:19). There *is* knowledge—for revelation is not irrational—but its object is precisely that love that, when recognized, is recognized as being of its very essence beyond knowledge. And as for the "fullness", it fills us in such a way that, far from filling God into us, we are filled up into God.

Here, then, identification cannot be partial, only total: the unqualified surrender to the love of Christ that we know to be beyond knowledge. Conditional surrender, faith with reservations—these are self-contradictory. From Abraham to Jesus (who always challenges the whole person to respond in faith), the essence of faith's surrender lies in putting objections to one side. Furthermore, we have seen that there can be no bodily Christ apart from his body, the Church, with its organs. They are one. So it is impossible to identify oneself totally with Christ and only partially with the Church.

But what about the actual Church and its scandals that cry to heaven: surely that cannot be the body of Christ! Surely everyone can see that the two do not fit! For conscience' sake I must at least choose between things that are acceptable and things that are intolerable. Is not practically everyone agreed nowadays that John XXIII exercised his primacy in a way that was acceptable, whereas his predecessor and successor did not?

It is a matter of principle. Unfortunately, there is only one Church, with as much historical reality as its Founder, and we cannot appeal to some better, ideal Church against the inadequacies and offences of the Church as it is. Unfortunately, we can only get hold of the ideal Church in the empirical Church. We have access to usage only in ill-usage, ab-use, which cannot be abolished but must be improved so that it can become credible and usable once again.

We have already said that the fullness of individual dogmas cannot function as a living body of truth if they are dissected and spread out for inspection. Does that mean that they are false? No, they are aspects and organs of a single truth to which they relate, and they must be read in the context of the latter. Nowadays, the aim is to carry out this work of integration by clear steps according to the various degrees of importance involved (the "hierarchy of truths"). It is a useful and illuminating procedure. But the principle cuts both ways and is dangerous[9] in that it allows the individual to determine what is central and what is peripheral for him. What is more, it fails to see that an aspect of the mystery that is quite central can light up something that seems peripheral. These are things that simply have to be seen. Perhaps what is needed is a deeper reflection, a greater familiarity with symphonic truth, if it is to be seen. Here, once again, the mind that is simple has the advantage over the theologian with his critical thought. The former sees intuitively straight through to the totality, trusting that the Church, in its meditation in faith, will not get lost in peripheral matters. The theologians check the details and are in danger of taking them as intelligible per se and of losing their connection with the Whole. Unfortunately, theologians are prone to spend so much time with details and their formulation that the sense of proportion is upset even in the case of the simple mind (for example, the manner of Christ's presence in the Eucharist). When this happens, we need once more to get in touch with the mystery by employing the criterion of maximality (of love's realism, not of the physics of the sacraments).

The same thing applies to Church office and discipline: the ideal is only to be found in the real, not behind it. It is impossible to circumvent our dependence on mediating office or to suspend it for a time. Many people who find the way office is exercised insufficiently evangelical, spiritual and ministerial en-

[9] Cf. I. F. Görres "Skelett oder Leib?" in *Im Winter wächst das Brot* (Einsiedeln, 1970).

deavor to follow their own ideas and do without the Church's mediation at all; they try to find a direct relationship to Christ that, historically and theologically, does not exist. They get into a no-man's-land, imagining that they are in a kind of overseas colony of Mother Church, but no longer recognizing the Church's priority over the Christian. It is not a case of judging people's subjective consciences here, but of uncovering an objective contradiction.

In many Christian countries, the "anti-Roman" attitude is regarded as fashionable. Rome, as a whole, is retrograde, not equal to the postconciliar situation, authoritarian and so forth. Whether or not such views are well-founded, the problem lies elsewhere: are those who hold them, and who are incensed at the clumsy exercise of authority, prepared to accept any office or authority exercised in the name of Christ? There will still be a number who are ready to submit to official authority if it is more Christlike and more worthy of belief, particularly if it speaks in its solemn, *ex cathedra* mode. Their antipathy is directed, not against the *cathedra,* but against its particular occupant. But this means that, in their view of the Church, the *cathedra* is abstract; their own submission is conditional and their whole approach has become that of an ideology of their own designing and subject to their own evaluation. They would submit, but not at present. Or else they submit grudgingly, which of course contradicts the real view of the Church put forward by Christ and the original apostles. They have a certain "symphony" in their mind's ear, but they refuse to play in the particular symphony being performed at present.

Were they to identify themselves with the mystery of Christ in the real Church, which shares his humiliation and his Cross and is continually being resurrected with him in the Spirit, they would bring their objections and reservations with them into this identification and consider how they might help to ameliorate the situation from within in whatever ways are open to them. In the body of Christ, nothing thrives except by the love of the members for one another. The particular member cannot perform its ministry unless it loves and is loved in return. This ministry may be that of admonishing and chastising in the Lord's name and with his authority. When humiliation is called for and imposed, revealing the Lord's Spirit, there can be no appealing against it to the freedom and maturity of members of the Church. True, it is the Lord of the Church himself who fashions his body to follow him in the discipleship of the Cross, but it is also the chief responsibility of the office he instituted to form the members after Christ's pattern and to suffer for the sake of this ministry (Gal 4:19). Office is a particular service of love, designed to help all to enter more deeply into their particular attitude of loving service. If they all look together at the head, the ministering Lord (Jn 13:13), there need never be any interruption in the dialogue between the disciples—whatever their special mission within the body may be—through their failing to understand each other, nor need such dialogue descend to bitterness. They all should identify themselves totally with the mystery of Christ, not only as it took place once in history for thirty-three years, but as this one same mystery takes place down through the ages and in the present. They are a part of the mystery; they cannot select aspects of it. In fact it is the mystery, whole and entire, that has elected them. They have all been taken prisoner for the sake of true freedom and must bear the other members, in all their differentness, with the forbearance that comes from the love that embraces them all: "I therefore, a prisoner for the Lord, beg you to lead a life worthy of the calling to which you have been called, with all lowliness and meekness, with patience, forbearing one another in love, eager to maintain the unity of the Spirit in the bond of peace. There is *one* body and *one* Spirit, just as you were called to the *one* hope that belongs to your call, *one* Lord, *one* Faith, *one* baptism, *one* God and Father of us all, who is above all and through all and in all" (Eph 4:1–6).

This should result in the members of the Church seeking to outdo each other in the depth and effectiveness of their grasp of the unity between the bodily and spiritual aspects, or between what is "visible" and "invisible" in the Church. This competition would have to take place in freedom, for no one can be a member of the Church except in freedom. But equally, no one can seek to put forward his freely evolved ideas as a substitute for *what* has been given to the Church by God in Christ. It is only the *how* of this emulation that is left free—how it is to be lived, in the unity of body and spirit and under the law of maximality of God's love, as a gift that calls for a response. Imagine that a bowling club is started in which the members agree to meet every fortnight for a game, to pay an annual fee and have an annual meeting and dinner; then someone says he wants to join while at the same time making it clear that he has no interest whatever in bowling, does not intend to pay the annual fee and finds annual meetings utterly boring. Such a person cannot expect to be accepted as a member, nor can he accuse the club of being intolerant and lacking in a sense of pluralism. Of course, this example limps at the crucial point, namely, the maximality of the Catholica, which is essentially unique and not to be compared with anything else.

Having said this, Christians should be continually and freely vying with one another in showing whether the "one Spirit" corresponds to the "one body", whether the Church's answer to its self-giving Lord is clear and wide enough, whether it is manifesting enough imagination (in the Holy Spirit) to respond to the astounding imagination of God in his self-surrender. Such competition, however, cannot alter, select or set aside anything of God's all-embracing work, nor can any response diverge from that of *ecce ancilla Domini*. That is the total answer that is expected: within the *one* body, the *one* baptism and the *one* Faith a partial answer is insufficient. Man has the right freely to involve himself in a partial way with all earthly plans and enterprises, for as long as he likes and for as long as he finds them meaningful. But God, who has involved himself totally on man's behalf, has the right to expect that those who have grasped the maximal nature of his involvement will at least attempt to identify themselves totally with him.

The criterion we have established applies to dogmatics. It shows that the multiplicity of approximate forms of expression is perfectly normal, indeed indispensable. The Christian has no cause for alarm at this plurality. The mystery itself, in its maximality, serves as the critical instance selecting and grading the formulas, and the Church's teaching office, supported by theology, allows itself to be guided by this criterion in its theoretical and practical instruction.

However, in another respect the mystery of Christ seems to open the floodgates to a pluralism that threatens to become uncontrollable. If Christ was one (and all Christologies must converge on this oneness of his), he apparently tolerated and even propounded a multiplicity of ethical attitudes, laying rigoristic requirements on some (primarily his disciples) while exhibiting an indulgent magnanimity toward others (the mass of the people, sinners). In reply we can say that these diverse attitudes on the part of Jesus all spring from the same center, from the new law of love, which on the one hand called for the old ethics of law to be internalized and thus made more radical (Mt 5:17–20 should then be seen in the light of 5:21–6:4) and on the other hand rejected all ethical pharisaism (Lk 18:9ff.), showing solidarity with the spiritual poverty of the "tax collectors and sinners" who had a more ready access to the way of love than did the hard-boiled strivers for perfection. That is true, and it shows that rigorousness and leniency go together in a single attitude, a single demand on Jesus' part. We can go further: his inclination toward "sinners" who are sick and need a physician presses him to seek out those who are not far from love (for the self-righteous are the worst sinners); but once the sinner has repented ("Go and sin no more!"), not only does he receive the blessings of love, but he must make them his own and therefore submit to the demands of selfless love. And this selfless love has to be unbending toward itself in order to be magnanimous with others. In this case, the ethics of Jesus would be a dynamic unity drawing the "periphery" toward the "center", but in which the same attitude is expressed vis-à-vis the periphery as in the centripetal movement.

This may be true, but what practical consequences will follow in the Church once the primitive Christian dream (that the Church consists of nothing but saints and the "perfect") has faded away?—once it is clear that there are many sinners in the Church, weighing it down like ballast, many people on the moral margins to whom a good Christian evidently must continue to be magnanimous, but who are not ready to be faced with the perfection of Christian love as a norm? Put very briefly, the Church can adopt two attitudes toward this difficult question.

It can erect the ethical ideal as the only normative goal and let it shine as a beacon above everyone, be they nearer to or more remote from love's perfection. The danger of this solution (and it can be substantiated by history) is that the particular demands made by Jesus of his disciples (leaving everything and following him, the renunciation of marriage, perfect obedience to him) are understood as the practical working out of this norm, and the lives of all other Christians are measured thereby. The ages that, it was thought, put forward a double standard of morality (one for better and one for ordinary Christians) are basically those in which people believed they could manage with a single morality, applied analogically.

The other solution is to permit a multiplicity of realizations in the name of the one, sole commandment of love. Clearly, the danger here is that, in practice, the state of life of the "Christian in the world" (as opposed to the Christian living by the evangelical counsels) gets closer to the state of those living on the Church's margin. In other words, the stringency of the one commandment of love changes imperceptibly into the tolerance of love in the face of manifold human weakness. It is at this point that there is the threat of a real ethical pluralism.

In addition, we must be aware that the world in which Christianity lives not only has highly pluralist views about good and evil, about what is permissible and what is not, but also is faced with problems of survival—for example, overpopulation—where the common good must take precedence over all private ethical points of view. The dangers to ethics posed by such decisions are clear, and the Church's teaching office can be subject to much soul searching in adopting these premises. In the same connection, a great number of Christians who in practice only partially identify themselves with the Church are in a situation of coexistence with an environment that neither thinks nor acts according to Christian ethics. The Church cannot simply set before these Christians the normative goal that applies to those whose identification is total (and toward which the latter have to strive with a living faith). Is the Church then to leave them to their own "consciences", merely helping them on their way with some humanistic notion of love or social awareness, but sparing them the specifically Christian norms and commandments? But in that case, how shall it draw the boundaries between the ethics for the "fully committed" and the ethics for the "partially committed"—especially since the sociological decisions regarding mankind and the general moral "climate" concern all Christians?

There are no ready-made solutions for these complex questions. However, a few guidelines can be given. In its early and middle period the Church was doubtless well-advised (by the Gospel) in prescribing the Christian perfection of love as the norm for everyone, and not as some vague social awareness but with the precise and hard conclusions of the Sermon on the Mount. The Church could (and should) do the same today, particularly as this unbending norm is accepted, at least as a desirable ideal, even by people who otherwise have litle time for detailed moral prescriptions. What was time bound was that this norm was realized (in an approximate way) in the closest connection with a particular form of Church life (that of the evangelical counsels). Even if, from the point of view of the New Testament, such a connection was not illegitimate —and in the Gospel itself the ideal of the Christian is drawn from actual, concrete discipleship (Lk 14:25ff.)—the very concreteness of this discipleship was itself subject to a spiritual norm, namely, that same selfless and perfect love that applied to all without distinction. Fundamentally, the Church has always known this. This spiritual norm, presupposed as valid for all, can be lived out in its wholeness in the various Christian forms of life (for example, virginity, marriage), even if a greater entanglement in the determinisms of the world can make it harder to practice pure Christian love. In order to cope with the complications that arise through Christians' personal and social involvement with secularity per se and in particular with their contemporary world, the teaching and guiding Church can and must issue certain guidelines. These will be all the more plausible and all the more willingly accepted, the more directly they mirror the love of Christ. But as we have seen, this love is indivisible, whether it is directed toward sinners who are to repent or toward the zealous who are trying to practice it. It is of the greatest importance that the Church's ethical guidelines should manifest this unity, which makes a harmful pluralism impossible by simultaneously calling "sinners" (Mt 9:13) and enjoining on disciples a "righteousness that exceeds that of the scribes and Pharisees" (Mt 5:20). It is this ethics that confronts men in their various situations in order to lead them to Christ and sends them out into the most diverse situations to live the one Christian life there under conditions that may differ drastically from one to another.

n. *Conclusion*

On our tour of theological pluralism, have we shirked the difficult area, the slippery slope? I do not think so. None of our situations can be as dire as Christ's—

whose impress is upon the lives of all of us. The ultimate and crucial test is the Cross, where God hides himself *sub contrario*. But at that point there is only suffering in an identity that is held fast through obedience; there is no longer any place for the complaint of Job, who accuses God of contradicting himself, no pattern for dispute within the Church.

It can be hard to carry out our task in the Church if we are alone with God and no one else understands. The only thing for it is to fight without moving an inch from the center of the mystery of Christ. We need cords and ropes of living, constant prayer to hold us to this center, for if we let go, the particular will triumph over our sense of unity, and our mission (which only has meaning within the unity) will be wrecked—yet again.

But what a tremendous panorama of freedom opens up for us from the vantage point of Christ's unity! "All things are yours", world, life and death, present and future, if "you are Christ's", for "Christ is God's" (1 Cor 3:21ff.). The whole door opens on a single pivot; the plurality of all the forms in the world and in history, including death and the future, is accessible to the Christian's thinking and acting, if indeed he surrenders himself with Christ to God. To God, who is everything and at the same time freely determines himself, and who, in the determinate shape of his Word, gives the world his All.

We think that God cannot do this. We feel that by being so determinate God must involve himself in limitation: Is not Jesus Christ only *one* possibility among thousands? We are mistaken: "for in him the whole fullness of deity dwells bodily" (Col 2:9). God's determinate will is never a part of him but always God himself, whole and entire. So the whole fullness of truth can lie in the determinate and particular dogma, and the whole fullness of faith, love and hope in the particular charism. Whatever is in touch with itself at its origin cannot fail to know itself in the pluralism of perspectives and missions that spring from that origin. At root level they all meet and communicate.

II. Illustrations

Unity in multiplicity is the most commonplace problem facing all philosophies and all our attempts to come to grips with daily life. Theology should not act as if—all of a sudden, in the last twenty-four hours—it had to bear the entire burden itself. Theology always has the task of showing that the living God is free enough to utter his most particular word in many languages.

The illustrations assembled here show how that unity, which manifests itself in teeming multiplicity, does not lose itself but rather establishes and proves itself. The selection given is arbitrary. It is not meant to set forth any system, nor (even less) a handy recipe.

All love delights in letting the beloved *be,* in every gesture and in changing moods, and in recognizing him afresh in them. This applies in a special way to that love that characterizes the Church.

1. *Church and world*

Are these two or one? John draws a sharp distinction: "I am not praying for the world but for those whom thou hast given me" (Jn 17:9). But shortly before this we read: "Thou hast given him power over all flesh" (Jn 17:2). And then: "I in them and thou in me, that they may become perfectly one, so that the world may know that thou hast sent me" (Jn 17:23). Multiple and categorical boundaries are drawn, only to be over-stepped in the same breath. How is Church to understand itself? Can it understand itself at all? Or, in understanding itself properly, must it not surrender all claim to a clearly delineated self-understanding? Indeed, must we not simultaneously intensify both aspects: the less Church is identical with world and the more it is itself, the more open and vulnerable it is to the world and the less it can be marked off from it? Can such a paradox be thought, let alone lived?

It must.

Illumination can only come through being joined to the body of Christ. By being joined, not by making a comparison. For the Church is not merely metaphorically the body of Christ, but by the power of the Eucharist it is that part of mankind that he has joined to his personal body in such a way that he lives in the Church as the soul lives in the body. The image is imperfect, for he has his own body; it exercises its being[1] within the body of the Church without dissolving and being subsumed into it, because his (eucharistic) body is a transfigured body that is no longer subject to the destiny of mortal things. All the same, it is Christ's body that opens up an understanding of the Church in the world.

The body of Christ is "my flesh for the life of the world" (Jn 6:51). If it is to nourish the world, all mankind, with divine life, it must be a body of inconceivable purity, of absolutely divine purity; it must really be the divine Word, implanted into this matter to imprint its unique form upon it. Even under the Old Covenant there was a foreshadowing of this materialization of the divine Word: "And he humbled you [Israel] and let you hunger and fed you with manna, which you did not know, nor did your fathers know; that he might make you know that man does not live by bread alone, but that man lives by everything that proceeds out of the mouth of the Lord" (Dt 8:3). Here the material manna is compared to a word issuing

---

[1] *Es West* [Tr.].

forth from the mouth of God. And Jesus explicity goes a step further than this prefiguring image: "Your fathers ate the manna in the wilderness, and they died. This is the bread which comes down from heaven, that a man may eat of it and not die. I am the living bread which came down from heaven" (Jn 6:48ff.). Christ's body is described, its meaning and being are made accessible, by reference to a movement coming from very high up and far away, down to the greatest possible breadth and depth. It is more a body for (the world) than a body with, juxtaposed to, other, self-contained bodies. One is reminded of the leaven in the parable that is mixed with the dough "until the whole is leavened".

This body needs no opening to the world; it is itself the opening that God has created for himself in order to enter into the world's material and historical reality, its destiny and becoming. The body is not only the opening but also that by which God enters, the veritable organ by which divine fruitfulness is sowed into the womb of mankind. From this perspective we can understand the virginity of this body, which must keep itself intact and continent so that, once and for all, it may pour forth as God's seed. We are always coming across the same law: original purity, continually welling up in Jesus' prayer to the Father, in his constant, absolute obedience in childlike love, so that it can exercise the greatest possible purifying and enlivening influence in the world. In being poured out for the world as Eucharist, the body seems to have totally surrendered its particular shape. This outpouring coincides with death on the Cross: "Unless a grain of wheat falls into the earth and dies, it remains alone; but if it dies, it bears much fruit" (Jn 12:24). "You foolish man! What you sow does not come to life unless it dies. And what you sow is not the body which is to be, but a bare kernel, perhaps of wheat or of some other grain. But God gives it a body as he has chosen" (1 Cor 15:36ff.). The comparison that is important here is not the biological process but the fact that the continuity of the bodily form is interrupted in the death phase. Indeed, the course of events is represented as if the dying grain had no guarantee that its decaying form would yield a new form of the same ("wheat or some other grain"), but as if it were simply God's good pleasure to determine what kind of thing should emerge from the deceased grain.

Paul's example can be reapplied to the christological context, and then it means that Christ's body, in dying, makes no demands of the Father as to the particular form in which it will be resurrected in the world. "I do not seek my own glory; there is One who seeks it" (Jn 8:50). Here this One is the Father; sometimes it is the Holy Spirit (Jn 16:14), whom the Father has sent out into the world with this commission; but Christ's body is so perfectly surrendered in death and the Eucharist that all movement of self-preservation, self-reflection and planning is alien to it. Now he is wholly what, from his very origin, he was and is: the fluid Word that issues from the mouth of God. In its fluidity, this Word has the power of total penetration, but it is the Holy Spirit who causes it to be received and become fruitful in the world's womb, in the uniting of

the divine "cell" and the human "ovum", in encounter
and fertilization.

2

This teaches us more than anything else about the
Church's situation. If Church is primarily the goal and
result of Christ's self-surrender—that is, it is that portion of the world that has initially "accepted him" and
"become children of God" (Jn 1:12)—this *goal* itself
immediately changes into a *means* whereby Christ's
body extends its eucharistic influence over the world.
For the Church is grasped by Christ; he fashions it
after himself and joins it to his body, which is "for the
life of the world". Thus the second-century Letter of
Diognetus can describe Christians as the soul of the
world, only slightly modifying Paul's picture in Phil
2:15, where he calls the Philippians "children of God
without blemish", shining like stars in the universe.
So, consistent with its goal, the Church is anything
but a closed sheep pen. In the Parable of the Shepherd,
in fact, the door (which Jesus also is) is opened, and the
sheep are let out individually; outside, in the world,
Jesus, the Shepherd, goes ahead of those who are his,
and there they recognize his voice (Jn 10:3f.). Accord-
ingly, the disciples are sent out, to "all nations" (Mt
28:18), "to the end of the earth" (Acts 1:8). Corresponding to its goal, therefore, Church only exists in
the dynamic mode, on all the roads of the world, but
from a theological point of view this vocation and
mission are not primarily an intramundane, sociologi-

cally ascertainable process (though at a secondary level it may evince such aspects), but a eucharistic process involved in the law of Christ's life—which is given to be shared out. Thus, Church will suffer the loss of its shape as it undergoes a death, and all the more so, the more purely it lives from its source and is consequently less concerned with preserving its shape. In fact, it will not concern itself with affirming its shape but with promoting the world's salvation; as for the shape in which God will raise it from its death to serve the world afresh, it will entrust it to the Holy Spirit. We have already observed[2] that nothing in the Church is exempt from death and destiny; there is no "structure" existing independently of the event of Christ. If Paul is suffering and in danger, "office" itself suffers and is threatened. It is God himself who guides his Church, with all its aspects, through the storms of time. However many founderings there may be, God will not permit the gates of hell to overcome it. This would be the place for a detailed commentary on the account of the shipwreck, full to the brim with symbolism, that concludes the inspired part of the history of the Church (Acts 27).

3

But this reality that, in exploding, is to bring forth such fruit must not be any random thing in the world, a possibility, an ideology, one idea among thousands. It must have become qualitatively what, in virtue of its

[2] Cf. Part one, section g.

origin—Christ—it already is and is to be, namely, the leaven that facilitates the ultimate unification of the world in its totality, the enzyme and organism of the eschatological salvation that has appeared in Christ. The Church's ambition of embracing the world's unity within its own is not arrogance but obedience to Christ in faith. The fact that this ambition, once openly proclaimed, provokes the scornful shrugging of shoulders (because the Church's external shape allows less and less of its catholicity to be seen; it appears to be just one denominational church among others and may soon seem to be an insignificant sect with few members)—this cannot shake its legitimacy.

It is the Church's task to gather the world together into a unity under the headship of Christ, thus offering the world that unity for which it is striving deliberately but clearly in vain. The movement toward world unification, which nowadays has evidently become an issue for the whole planet, suffers from a flagrant, twofold contradiction. The first is the fact that mankind is splitting progressively into two unequal halves, the smaller portion consisting of the exploiting countries with their high standard of living, and the larger portion of the exploited, poor and starving. Sociologically the Church is associated chiefly with the smaller bloc. But those of us who belong to it are nowadays experiencing a rapid disintegration of its *ethos*. Its very affluence produces ennui, boredom and the need for people to break out of this artificial world, whether by means of intoxication, ecstasy or the anarchistic destruction of present reality irrespective of what may take its place. In facing the first problem, the

Church has to show solidarity with the poor and exploited, both by proclaiming the personal worth of every human being and, where possible, by denouncing and attacking the system of economic exploitation. In former times, various elites in the Church always gave succor to the poor, the powerless, the desolate, prisoners, children and the aged, the sick and the dying. Now this work is to be promoted both theoretically and practically as something involving everyone, at a global level, as Christianity's proper concern, arising from the Catholic awareness of the unity of mankind in Christ.

The second task is even harder. Teilhard de Chardin was right when he sensed its contemporary challenge: the development of human freedom reaches the point where mankind can no longer see any reason for pressing further and is tempted to destroy itself and the world. In such a situation, only Christians will have a reason to keep going, a reason they can share with others; only they will have the courage to pursue the path of history. But how can this reason, which only becomes visible to faith, be made clear to our despairing and discouraged contemporaries? The example of life is the best recommendation, by showing solidarity with those in revolt against the establishment and, by building on their justified criticism of it and on their goodwill, demonstrating to them that Christianity is more than a moral code (namely, it is spontaneous love) and more than an imposed order (namely, it is a love that creates order from within in absolute freedom).

All this having been done, however, there can be no promise of unqualified success. It is beyond the power of Christians (unless there is a total catastrophe) to remove the causes of these problems—chiefly the accumulation of technological affluence. As the "one world" becomes increasingly more questionable it will be their task to put forward the idea of the "one salvation" in a way that people can believe in. Where is it written that the evolution, in which Christians are involved and which puts into man's hands increasing power over things, must inevitably lead to the best of all possible states of affairs? Can it? Christians are the only ones, in this mushrooming development, who can confront it with a divine plan of salvation that is coextensive with it, indeed that always runs ahead of it because it is eschatological. This divine plan contains the whole apocalyptic explosion and provides it with a meaning. That is why Christians are not fundamentally disturbed in the face of the apocalyptic dimension; they are familiar with it from holy Scripture, which, while it speaks of men on earth "passing away with fear", also mentions the rejoicing in heaven over the harvest gathered in from the world. If the Church has to squander itself prodigally in the world, giving itself eucharistically to be shared out with the result that its very shape disappears in ruins, it is able to see the collapse of the world, whose form is also passing away, as a destiny it shares; it will be able to speak words of hope to the sinking world.

4

However, all this presupposes most definitely that the shape of the Church, which is to be dissolved in fruitfulness, is there in the first place, and not as something vague and polymorphous, but as something that is clearly defined. "Everything depends on this: in order to *do,* one needs to *be*" (Goethe). The Church must be open to the world, yes: but it must be the *Church* that is open to the world. The body of Christ must be this absolutely unique and pure organism if it is to become all things to all men. That is why the Church has an interior realm, a *hortus conclusus, fons signatus* (a walled garden, a sealed spring), so that there *is* something that can open and pour itself out.

This is the context in which real contact and intercourse with Christ, the source who pours himself out and imprints his character on us, belongs—above all in that real contact and encounter that we call sacrament. Sacraments are gestures and gifts from Christ to us. We are primarily recipients, and only because we have received are we in a position to give to others. All sacraments sanctify with a view to the sacrifice that the Church and Christians have to make in giving themselves for the world. They are all involved with renunciation; they arise out of the renunciation of the Cross and are given to strengthen and refine our renouncing love. Being baptized means being privileged to die with Christ, "being buried into his death", removed from all temporal reality, so that we can be sent back into it purged of evil desire. By doing penance and making confession of sin we are continually saying Yes to the challenge to take up our cross daily and be disciples. The Eucharist "proclaims the death of the Lord": it is the reception of his crucified love in the heart of the Church and our response to it in our readiness to be sacrificed along with it. The sacrament of matrimony even subordinates *eros* to renouncing, selfless love, *agape;* priestly ordination is a "consecration in truth" together with the Lord (Jn 17:19) as a sacrifice for the world. It is above all for this intimate communion with the Lord's life, mind and heart that "office" exists in the Church. It is a means of communication between the Lord and those who are his, and in such a way that the very person and existence of the one mediating it can be rendered transparent, allowing the subject of his mediation to shine through. This same transparency is to characterize the situation where Church office has to pronounce the Lord's truth and carry out his instructions in the life of the community and of the individual. Church office, at its root, is the most esoteric element in the Church's internal life: it does not face outward at all, does not represent Christianity to the world—this is done by individual Christians when they step out into the world—but rather is designed to keep open the believers' direct access to the original sources of salvation *ex latere Christi*. Even if every Christian is able to take up holy Scripture, ponder and pray it, Scripture itself is not primarily something "taken" but rather something "given". Even if every Christian can directly discern the voice of the Holy Spirit in his conscience, we do not "take" the Spirit. We are given a share in him to the extent that we are continually being incorporated afresh into the Church, where he "apportions to each one individually as he wills" (1 Cor 12:11).

As Paul's letters clearly show, Church office ultimately guarantees that the Christians' love for one another, which is intended to make the Church the model of unity for the world (Jn 13:35; 17:23), will not become closed in on itself in the manner of a sect. Church office explodes all complacent charismatic notions (such as those of the Corinthians) and opens them up to the Catholic horizon of Christ's self-denying love. That is absolutely crucial. If the measure of love within the Church were the experience of reciprocal commitment, common religious experience, shared enthusiasm for the cause of Christ and so forth, there would soon be a pact among the "pneumatics" against the "fleshly Christians", or, in Paul's terms, the "strong" against the "weak". Such a division within the community would create a pneumatic sect, which can never provide a Catholic model for the world's unity. In order to be a model of this kind, Christians must have passed the test, within the Church itself, of a love that renounces experience. They must have attained that experience of love that manifests itself precisely in and through renunciation (just as a good marriage can only be regarded as having proved itself when *agape* has taken a sufficiently deep root through renunciation of the egoisms of *eros*). It is Church office that wrests the individual's own criteria from him and hands them over to the Lord of the Church, guaranteeing that the Church's experience of love shall transcend itself in the direction of the love of Christ (as Head of the Church) and shall overcome all its subjectivisms and attain the objectivity of that love that "believes all things, hopes all things, endures all things" (1 Cor 13:7).

This is where pluralism in the Church is really at

home, where it is not merely tolerated as an evil but called for as a highest good. Here I respect the other as what he is, without being in tune with him at the level of experience, but as someone with whom I must get along in the ecclesial body of Christ. There is a harmony between us, but it is only objective, not experienced: "Who are you to pass judgment on the servant of another? It is before his own master that he stands or falls. And he will be upheld, for the Master is able to make him stand" (Rom 14:4). The Petrine primacy has its ultimate functional justification here, where it is a question of the catholicity of love: it gathers up the Church's entire endeavor toward transcendence and brings it to the Lord as a single response (cf. Jn 21:11).

Nowadays people are largely unaware of these truly esoteric things. The attempt to explain them in purely sociological terms is bound to fail. Then a faith that has become fainthearted clings to spiritual experiences; groups come into being in which such shared "Church experiences" are cultivated; but since there is no official structure to gather them up and set them in order, they are isolated in a vacuum and disintegrate as soon as the "experiences" get stale. The false opposition between spirit and structure must be overcome: in a living body the structural arrangement of the members is a function of the soul (Eph 4:16). The skeleton, the system of muscles and nerves cannot be set against the life process as mere institution. In the body of the Catholic Church, the only enduring Church experience is where people allow all their individual pneumatic experiences to be transposed into experiences of renunciation in the whole edifice of the Church. On this basis, genuine group experience can be legitimate. Indeed, by representing the whole, it can show a model of Catholic unity to the world.

5

Thus, every aspect of the Catholica that is visible and structural, seen in its proper perspective, is in the service of ecclesial love. The purpose of this love is to provide the exclusive model in which the world can recognize its own unity, a unity for which it strives but that it never succeeds in finding. If this were the Church's image, there would not need to be so much talk about changing its structures and about its (poor) prospects in the present and the future. But if new life is to flow into the members, it is not primarily a question of changing structures. They only need to be understood in their proper function, and then they will be able once more to minister to love. For love alone is the shape that is meant to strike the world: "By this all men will know that you are my disciples, if you have love for one another" (Jn 13:35). It is a love that has no self-promoting form; it does not arise like an artistic masterpiece before the eyes of spectators. It is the artless, spontaneous result of selflessness on the part of many. In this way it prefigures that formlessness in which the Church, crucified in the world, is to lay down its life.

The way in which Christians are to emerge from the love that surrounds them in the Church, stepping out into the world in order to bear witness in their lives to the love of Christ, is not something that can be reduced to a simple formula. It exhibits a whole spectrum, reaching from the hidden holocaust of a Carmelite nun, who gives her life for the salvation of the world and the care of the most abandoned, to aggressive involvement in public life, in economics and politics on behalf of human rights and human dignity. Testimony to the Church's love can be borne by the individual, who seeks to spread to those around him the *communio* that is lived in the Church, and also by groups that collaborate to try to make its reality take root in the world. It is part of the approach of Catholic apostolic action to want to work together with non-Catholics, non-Christians and atheists in all things that promote the unification of mankind. Witness to the Spirit who inhabits the Church can be given through collaboration in cool, deliberate, expert planning in all departments of secular life just as much as through the unpredictable eruption of prophetical energies, bursting forth from the hidden regions where man communes with God.

Prophets should never be lacking in a Church that prays and is joined to its Lord in the Holy Spirit. It is not true that we cannot get saints by praying and practicing penance for them. What is true is that such prayer and penance must be characterized by holiness, a holiness that may perhaps be completely hidden. Furthermore, it is true that there is nothing more fruitful and more reformative in the Church than the presence of genuine holiness and prophesy. It breaks down the prejudices that people continually erect around the institutional aspect of the Church, effortlessly showing its transcendental significance. It is a nursery of new holiness in the Church—the emergence of a great saint causes holiness to spread like the ever-widening ripples in a pool. Think of Basil, Benedict, Francis, Ignatius, John of the Cross, Charles de Foucauld. Wherever genuine renewal is taking place, quietly and deeply, in today's Church, the movement can be traced back to an outpouring from a prophetical, charismatic or mystical wellspring. Such renewal may not get into the limelight; it may not fit in with the current catch phrases. But the Holy Spirit knows what a particular age's most pressing need is far better than men with their "programs".

The person who is commissioned by and obedient to the Spirit will preserve a sense of proportion in his task. Even if it is to be carried out on a broad canvas with a degree of exposure, he will not get lost in fantasy and abstraction. Noisy protests against war and famine in foreign lands and demagogic calls for the whole economic system to be changed are less effective than the quiet attention to what lies at hand, the conscientious development of real competence and the selfless investment of oneself—and not at a tentative and dilettante level—where the need is greatest. Through all this, there is a Providence that makes sure that the disproportion between the Goliath of the world powers and the Christian David remains a graphic one. It is not appropriate for David to strut around in the armor plating of power, wielding the instruments of world economics and politics, and bringing the ship onto a new course for the Kingdom of God on earth. "People do not expect us to win, but to offer resistance" (Claudel).

Like its Lord, then, the Church offers resistance with all its human resources: with its childlikeness in opposition to the world's false maturity before God; with the sagacity of adulthood, employing all the powers of the Spirit against the spirit that is hostile to God; with the wisdom of age, for which nothing more is needed than "abiding in love"; and particularly with the impotence of the death process, which it can turn into the most powerful witness to the love that transcends all things. "Arming in the Spirit" is quite different from arming in the flesh. The front line in which these weapons are used is likewise very different. Even when they are working together to eradicate suffering, the world is fighting for quality of life, whereas the Church is fighting for salvation. The quality of life and the happiness of the majority are in the forefront, while behind them there is still the unconquered fact of death. Salvation, however, embraces man and the world in their total destiny, which will only achieve fullness beyond time and beyond death. The unity of the world is continually falling apart in death, but the Church's unity, which adumbrates the unity of the coming Kingdom, gathers up the world's fragile unity—but in doing so it surrenders itself to that death that its Lord has already overcome.

2. Believing and doing

I

All that needs to be said about believing and doing has already been said by the Gospel. "A bad tree cannot produce good fruit. Not every one who says to me, 'Lord, Lord', shall enter the Kingdom of Heaven, but he who does the will of my Father who is in heaven." "Go and do likewise." "If you continue in my word, you are truly my disciples, and you will know the truth, and the truth will make you free." "A man had two sons; and he went to the first and said, 'Son, go and work in the vineyard today.' And he answered, 'I will not'; but afterward he repented and went. And he went to the second and said the same; and he answered, 'I go, sir', but did not go. Which of the two did the will of his father? They said, 'The first.' "— And the continuation is worth noting in our present context: "Jesus said to them, 'Truly, I say to you, the tax collectors and the harlots go into the Kingdom of

God before you. For John came to you in the way of righteousness, and you did not believe him, but the tax collectors and the harlots believed him; and even when you saw it, you did not afterward repent and believe him.'" And a final quotation to complete the circle: "'What must we do, to be doing the works of God?' Jesus answered them, 'This is the work of God, that you believe in him whom he has sent.'"

A circle is described here, in which believing and doing, orthodoxy and orthopraxy, are continually proceeding out of and returning to each other.

1. First of all, it is clear that God does not recognize a faith that produces no works, even if the believer were to prophesy in the name of Jesus, drive out demons and perform many miracles (Mt 7:22). So the kind of action that is expected of faith is something totally different from these apparently super-Christian works. The end of the Parable of the Good Samaritan, "Go and do likewise" (Lk 10:37), shows the thrust of that action that comes from faith.

2. However, when John speaks of "continuing in the word" (Jn 8:31f.), which leads to a knowledge of the truth and to freedom, his "continuing", while it is certainly a doing, does not follow the law of cause and effect. It is an inner dimension; it is the life of faith itself. Paul speaks of "faith working through love" (Gal 5:6).

3. The Parable of the Two Sons seems to introduce a contrary idea. Up to now, doing flowed from believing. Now faith is crossed out, as it were, in the son's refusal to obey, and we are left with doing, which now bears the weight and the proof of faith. Let us notice

that the son does not go to his work in an attitude of revolt, but rather after he has had a change of heart. In what follows, in the context of the tax collectors and harlots, this change of heart is described as faith. The high priests and elders whom Jesus is addressing here poured scorn on this change of heart, which they had seen with their own eyes; they refused to change themselves (Mt 21:28–32). So, while orthopraxy takes precedence here, it is by no means a merely external activity: it is action that has decided to follow the "way of righteousness" that John brought, a way that is recognized even by the son who said No.

4. Ultimately orthopraxy penetrates to the inner core of orthodoxy, yet in such a way that the work in view has God, not for its object, but for its subject. As for man's faith—his decisive "achievement"—it comes about when the believer acknowledges the divine "work" in himself and allows it to take effect (Jn 6:28f.). Thus orthodoxy is God's orthopraxy, making the believer's "doxy"[1] the affirmation of and participation in God's "praxy", *praxis*.

2

Right from the beginning, therefore, we are moving along a kind of circular track that, while it grants us a multiplicity of perspectives, excludes every rigid either/or and makes it impossible to absolutize a particular position. The either/or would be a faith without action, a doing without believing. There is no

---

[1] "Worship", from Greek *doxa*, "glory" [Tr.].

room for this, either in the Old or in the New Testament, in Paul or in James. Both apostles agree that everything flows from the attitude of Abraham, whose faith was not a mere "believing as true" but a total surrender to the all-giving and all-disposing God. Like Paul, we may include in the total concept of faith the disciple's obedient action and see love as flowing from it quite naturally and inevitably, or we may make a clearer distinction between the element of works and that of basic faith and declare that the former is necessary to complete the latter and render it effective (James 2:20ff.). But both elements together form man's response to God's grace. It is a living response, however: its inner aspects are in dynamic relation; each elicits the other and causes it to sally forth, only to return to a fresh embrace, in a ceaseless circular movement similar to that which lovers experience. The lover allows his partner freedom to "be" and in doing so becomes truly himself. Then there is a return to the wellspring of personal autonomy that lies in the gift of love of the beloved person. Let us review the four perspectives once more, remembering that they are not sharply separated from one another but are only markers on a constantly moving circular path.

1. Faith unaccompanied by corresponding action is dead. From the Synoptic Gospels, it is clear that the first thing to be "done", inherent in faith, is the decision not to resist God and to trust totally and in self-surrender in God's "work" in Jesus. Being "of little faith" is having faith without the courage to follow it up in terms of life. This courage can definitely be experienced as a grace and can be prayed for as such ("I

believe; help my unbelief!", Mk 9:24), but that does not alter the fact that it must be a response reaching out for God from the core of man's being.

Both Old and New Testaments campaign against man's tendency to find substitutes for this total act, which to sinful sloth seems not only troublesome but even dangerous. The favorite substitutes are, on the one hand, cultic worship and on the other, wisdom ("*gnosis*", biblical erudition, "theology" conceived as knowing all about God and the way he acts). God, however, despises a worship that is not the bodily expression of a devoted heart: "Behold, to obey is better than sacrifice, and to hearken than the fat of rams" (1 Sam 15:22). "For I desire steadfast love and not sacrifice, the knowledge of God, rather than burnt offerings" (Hos 6:6). "For thou hast no delight in sacrifice . . . a broken and contrite heart, O God, thou wilt not despise" (Ps 51:16f.). This applies just as much in Christ's Church as in the synagogue. The passive listening to sermons, the merely habitual frequenting of the Lord's table or going to confession and so forth are only partial gestures. They need to be integrated into the believer's whole life if they are to be meaningful and fruitful. Similarly, theology (understood as the Christian continuation of the learning of the scribes) must be backed up by life. This applies with equal force to the general form in which theology appears in the Church and to the individual theologian or any believer who is trying to acquire an intellectual understanding of faith. In each case there is a balance, to be continually borne in mind and to be striven for, between understanding and life. If the theology of a particular age is one-sidedly intellectualist and is not clearly matched, right down to its details, by an existential attitude of faith, it will not be apt to fit in as one element in the Christian life synthesis. In that case it will have to be melted down and recast into a new form more appropriate to its origin and thus provide a better model for Christian conduct. The Christian understanding of faith (*sophia:* 1 Cor 2:6; *gnosis:* 8:1–7) proves to be genuinely animated by the Holy Spirit when it manifests the pneumatic inventiveness of Christian love and reveals itself in pluriform expressions. In his letters, Paul scatters this pluriformity of love-in-action as if from a horn of plenty; he seems to broadcast them almost at random, and one has the impression that he could go on indefinitely. Let us listen to him:

"Let love be genuine; hate what is evil, hold fast to what is good; love one another with brotherly affection; outdo one another in showing honor. Never flag in zeal, be aglow with the Spirit, serve the Lord. Rejoice in your hope, be patient in tribulation, be constant in prayer. Contribute to the needs of the saints, practice hospitality. Bless those who persecute you; bless and do not curse them. Rejoice with those who rejoice, weep with those who weep. Live in harmony with one another; do not be haughty, but associate with the lowly; never be conceited. Repay no one evil for evil. . . . If possible, so far as it depends upon you, live peaceably with all. Beloved, never avenge yourselves. . . . If your enemy is hungry, feed him; if he is thirsty, give him drink . . ." (Rom 12:14ff.).

This was preceded by Paul's instruction on the unity

of the body and the multiplicity of ministries exercised by its individual members, according to the "measure" *(metron)* and the "proportion" (*analogia:* Rom 12:3, 6) of faith given to the individual. For Paul, the content of faith is naturally identical—God's action in Christ—but this faith is so existential in each Christian that it is "apportioned" to him by God in a completely personal way, so that the whole faith of the Church is reflected (proportionally, "analogically") in each personal vocation. And precisely because each vocation is specialized so close to its source—so that, as far as the believer is concerned, no grace is given apart from a mission that it imparts and nourishes—all Christian "doing" has a marked quality of thanksgiving (1 Th 5:18; Eph 5:20; Col 1:12, etc). No heteronomy can gain a foothold here: all Christian activity proceeds from faith, from the principle of that freedom that God has given us in his grace. Nor is this principle called into question when Church authorities or individual Church members initiate action in a Christian spirit (for example, the collection for the poor Jerusalem community: 2 Cor 8–9); there is enough scope for everyone to participate according to his own resources and degree of concern. All the same, each one is expected to know how to integrate his personal charism into the activity of the whole body, which is animated by a single blood circulation of faith and action.

It is clear that the word "commandment" has an entirely different ring to it in the New Covenant as compared with the Old (and also as compared with any system of morality). We can see this in the fact that Jesus, who is in no way subject to any extrinsic authority, speaks of himself as having a "commandment" or "charge" from the Father (Jn 10:18; 12:49f.). He understands the "new commandment" that he gives to his disciples (Jn 13:34) in the same way, as a "being one" with his mind ("just as I . . .": 15:10): the Christian operates in love and in accord with its "law", out of the fullness of love that he has received.

2. If we look at things in this perspective, it is quite easy to see the connection between "abiding" in the abundant wellspring and "going forth" into particular action. Those who import an artificial tension into this relationship forget that two people can love each other sincerely and yet both go out to pursue their respective daily occupations. The lover is accompanied by the thought of his beloved in a way that does not impede him in his work—in fact it sustains it. When he takes a break from work, the habitual thought of the beloved becomes actual and all his "distracting" daily work gathers around the center formed by this love. The example is inadequate, for the region whence faith springs, the source from which the Christian lives, is far more original, more profound, more universal and fruitful than any individual love relationship. This is the ambience in which every religious person tries to live, because it alone can impart enough meaning and enough power to support us as we try to carry out one single life's work in the world. But only the man of the Bible can experience it as the realm of eternally welling love; only he finds that the dichotomy between religion and the everyday round, between sacred and profane, between contemplation and action is already overcome, because in Jesus Christ the source of God's

love continually pours forth, active, into the world. Moreover, this love has risked the ultimate: it has put itself in the place of every last sinner and for his sake.

So the person who, in John's words, "continues in my word", "abides in my love", does not abandon himself to some kind of inert meditation, remote from the world, but—if he understands his faith aright—conducts his existence where the current of action is at its strongest, at the locus of God's initiative for the world, which absolutely requires the involvement in it of the one who "abides". In calling God's initiative to mind, he is not side by side with the object of his contemplation but actually within it, in such a way that he is filled by it: "Abide in me, and I in you" (Jn 15:4); "He who abides in me, and I in him" (15:5); "If you abide in me, and my words abide in you" (15:7); "All who keep his commandments abide in him, and he in them" (1 Jn 3:24); "God's nature ["seed"] abides in him" (1 Jn 3:9). This christological reciprocity is ultimately based on a trinitarian reciprocity: "If you keep my commandments, you will abide in my love, just as I have kept my Father's commandments and abide in his love" (Jn 15:10). Because the tension between abiding and going forth, love and obedience, contemplation and action has been overcome in Christ, it can be so in us too, through him.

"Abiding"—meaning faith, receiving in constant thankfulness, the amazed realization of the superabundance of divine gifts, the attempt to understand as much of it as possible—such abiding is both the continual spur to right action and its regulating principle. Without this "abiding", once faith had perceived the gift of God, our action would be inclined to rush around trying to make an appropriate response to God's initiative through compulsive, overhasty undertakings and attempts to change the world. That would be "works" in the sense in which Jesus and Paul reject them. God is not in a hurry in Jesus Christ, and the Christian's response is not meant to be hurried either. "He who believes will not be in haste" (Is 28:16). Of course, this does not mean that a disciple of Christ should not exert himself to the limit of his powers—no saint ever "took things easy". Many, such as Peter Claver or Francis Xavier, did so much that it seems a miracle that their strength was renewed, enabling them to go on working. They were overstretched, but this took place within a measure allotted to them. It was not something they adopted: they were challenged by it as something that came to them from their very origin. This "abiding" may devour them, yet it manifests a calm and a peace that indicates God's nearness. This applies to active lives as well as to contemplative. The latter, animated by a living faith, are as a rule more "devoured" than the former—their whole purpose is to be burnt up like blazing torches in God and by God, for his sake and for the sake of his work.

Fundamentally, "abiding" signifies the primacy of reception over response and transmission. In Christian terms this means the primacy of *logos* over *ethos*. The primary reception of the divine *Logos* (who manifests his love for the world in a normative manner) guarantees the primacy of faith's unity in the face of the multiplicity of action and infuses this multiplicity with the unity that binds everything together.

3. This raises the question of how far this unity needs to articulate itself consciously. Are Christians the only ones who act according to God's law? Do not other religions, world views and ethical stances contain a norm that, under one name or another (or even remaining more or less anonymous), regulates human conduct and makes it practically equivalent to Christian conduct? Do not both Christians and non-Christians work together under this generalized norm for the good of the state and for humanity as a whole? Why did Jesus specifically choose a "heretic"—one of the partially identified, we might say—a Samaritan, for the parable of neighborly love? Surely this explicitly separates the norm of *ethos* from the *logos* of true belief and sets the former above the latter? Surely this makes orthopraxy the norm of orthodoxy? And are we not compelled, in virtue of God's desire to save the whole world and to pour grace out for all, to speak of "anonymous Christians", especially as Jesus not only says, "He who is not with me is against me" (Mt 12:30), but also, "He that is not against us is for us" (Mk 9:40)? John, who shows a particular interest, at the end of his Gospel, in establishing the boundaries of the Petrine Church, had suggested that someone who cast out demons in the name of Jesus but did not wish to join the band of disciples should be stopped from exercising his gift. Jesus said No: "Do not forbid him; for no one who does a mighty work in my name will be able soon after to speak evil of me."

Here we have an indication of how to proceed even in cases where there is no explicit reference to Jesus, but where people act while distancing themselves from the Church. Albeit the basis on which such a person is operating is not acknowledged to be God's act in Jesus, it is bound to be some principle that he recognizes as normative and lasting. He will not "soon after" leave it behind and speak derogatively of it. So it was in the Parable of the Two Sons: the "orthopractician", who rebelled initially against his father's authority, pondered his position and recognized the binding quality of his father's wish, and this enabled him to carry it out. He goes to work in the vineyard, not because it suits him, but because his conscience afflicts him and he changes his decision in accordance with his father's wish (*metamelomai* Mt 21:30, 32). John the Baptist presented people with the "way of righteousness"; they submitted to it, acknowledged him and changed their former ways of life to take up the new one. Many people encounter a "way of righteousness" in their conscience, in a norm that arises within their life's horizon as the best guideline possible for them, and which they follow at some cost to themselves. Following such a path involves a certain submission, a certain obedience. And if they turn aside from this path, they do so with a certain regret that they are too weak to pursue it further. They are quite clear about one thing: this norm does not coincide with their desires or with what suits them. And even if they were to suggest that man proposes this norm for the sake of his own happiness, that it is *his* creation, they themselves are not "man" in general but some particular individual, submitting more or less reluctantly to this norm, the norm of "man" or of "humanity". They do not create the norm but act in accordance with a good that is laid on the individual and makes it possible for human beings to live together; they act in accordance with a good that the individual *expects* of his fellowmen, so that he too may respond to their expectation of him. It is this common basis that enables Christians to work together with non-Christians. "So whatever you wish that men would do to you, do so to them; for this is the law and the prophets" (Mt 7:12). We expect the good, we hope for the best that is possible, from our fellow men. Only the Christian knows the extent of that good given to him from God through the man Jesus Christ, a good that has become the norm of his conduct. It is something he can try to communicate to his fellowmen, with whom he is working together for the good of humanity.

4. Ultimately, the difference between believing and doing is almost obliterated. The more a Christian becomes aware of the norm that is represented by what God has effected in and for him, the more this norm pervades all his own actions. The two things go hand in hand: he himself is impelled to activate all his energies—and his own achievements seem less and less significant compared with the shining norm that pervades everything. On the one hand, he does all that he can; on the other, he allows the norm to wield its own power. He only needs to part with all the (often deeply hidden) resistance within him to this norm—which, in Christian terms, is the love of God—and the best possible "achievement" will take place within him. God acts in and through him, both in his intense effort and when he is completely relaxed and recovering his strength. Christianity is not the only religion to recog-

nize this as a universal scheme of perfection. Indian and Chinese wisdom, for example, Zen Buddhism, are also aware of it, under the heading of a negative theology that allows the Wholly Other to take precedence over all man's being and doing and seeks to let this precedence assert itself more and more. Many ideological aspects can obscure the respect for the Absolute that is latent here, yet it cannot be entirely extinguished. Thus the Christian shares certain insights with non-Christians, right up to and including this ultimate, mysterious identity of "doing" and "not-doing"—which is represented by the Christian's acting in total receptivity to God's initiative. Yet it is only in Christianity that this ultimate mystery of human orthopraxy is clearly and finally manifested in a way that brings the greatest bliss: here it is no longer a precondition for action that one must project oneself into the void, beyond the realm of the knowable. Instead it is the overfulfillment of one's hope for love, a hope that man always cherishes vis-à-vis his fellowmen, that results in action. For the love that my fellowman Jesus Christ gives me is much more than what one human being can give another. It is the effective pledge, the prolonging of God's absolute love into our world. And through the gift of the Holy Spirit, who is poured out into our hearts, I am enabled to offer myself so that the love of God can take effect in the world through me. When this receptivity and availability become a reality, believing and doing are perfected in each other and become one. Faith becomes instrumental and action attracts belief.

3. "A God at hand, a God afar off"—the absences of Jesus

God's presence in and absence from the world are a mystery that is impenetrable to thought and even more so to man's senses and experience. It would seem that we can only think and speak of it in propositions that are dialectical, that is, which cancel each other out. For if we construct the idea of God as its content demands, God is both everything (*to pan estin autos*: Sir 43:27)— for nothing can be outside God, nor can anything be added to him—and "exalted above all his works" (*para panta ta erga autou*: Sir 43:28). For none of these works is God: indeed, each of them is separated from him by the infinite distance and opposition of absolute and relative. The more God has to be in all things if they are to "be" at all, the more his presence in them reveals him to be utterly different from them: the more he is immanent, the more he is transcendent. This dialectic is correct in its own particular way, but it sounds empty; religious experience finds it hard to follow, with the result that the images of God in the religions manifest a pluralist diversity.

No one has ever seen the Father, but the Son has "interpreted" him (Jn 1:18) in human form. As the Word-made-flesh, he has clothed the ineffable in human categories, but in such a way that the essentially incomprehensible God can be discerned shining through and beyond all these categories of comprehensibility. However, since the picture of Jesus manifests a clear profile that can be grasped by our senses, in faith, he unites in himself, concretely, the plurality of divergent notions of God. God, ever incomprehensible, approaches us as a "God at hand", yet he would not be God if he were not also a "God afar off" (Jer 23:23). Jesus would not be truly the Word, revealing the Father to us, if he introduced us only to the Father's immanence and not his transcendence as well. Moreover, taking his whole life together, he reveals these two aspects simultaneously, just as God is simultaneously above and in us, both near and far, understood and exceeding our grasp. For in Jesus, "we see our God made visible and so are caught up in love of the God we cannot see" (Preface of Christmas I). God himself does not somehow hold the balance between immanence and transcendence; his total immanence proclaims to us his ever-greater transcendence. On the basis of his transcendence, of his being God-in-himself, he becomes immanent in the creature, bending down in grace and faithfulness, and in the eternal Covenant, to us who are almost nothing.

This is illustrated in the way Jesus' constant abiding with us is realized in and through periods when, increasingly, he withdraws and is absent. It is almost as if his coming into the world is only so that he can disappear: "Again, I am leaving the world and going to the Father" (Jn 16:28). But this "going to the Father" is in fact the way he returns to them or stays with them. "You heard me say to you, 'I go away, and I will come to you.' If you loved me, you would have rejoiced, because I go to the Father" (Jn 14:28). And he gives two reasons for this. First, as he immediately adds, "for the Father is greater than I": in disappearing and going to "God who is greater", Jesus himself attains his full stature—which was glimpsed on the Mount of Transfiguration and will become final at the Resurrection. The disciples must show that their love is genuine by desiring him to attain this form rather than stay in the transitory form, accessible to sense experience, which he adopted for love of them and in which they experience him as the-One-who-is-present. The other reason is this: "I tell you the truth: it is to your advantage that I go away, for if I do not go away, the Counselor will not come to you; but if I go, I will send him to you" (16:7). In other words, this latter mode of God's presence, the Spirit of Father and Son, can come about only through the withdrawal of the sensible presence of the Son—indeed, only if the disciples explicitly affirm this withdrawal. It is bound to be painful for man, who relies on his senses, but Jesus expects the pain of this renunciation to be outweighed by love for him and for his perfecting in God: spiritual joy cannot be gained without the pain of renunciation. That is why he reproaches them: "But now I am going to him who sent me; yet none of you asks me, 'Where are you going?' But because I have said these things to you, sorrow has filled your hearts" (16:5f.). Truly he will come back to them with the Spirit; there are many express promises that he will return (Jn 14:3, 21, 23, 28; 16:16; cf. Mt 18:20; 28:20). But now his (real) presence is a pneumatic one—which is exactly the case in the Eucharist—and hence a presence that presupposes that he be absent to the senses.

However, it is not as if the Incarnate One's presence on earth were one-sidedly under the sign of bidding farewell and disappearing. Such a view would make him almost some kind of gnostic pseudobeing who did not really touch the earth's surface and was never really acquainted with the realities of bodily existence. On the contrary, the life of Jesus is full of immediate, tangible closeness. He is particularly near to the "tax collectors and sinners" with whom he habitually dines, to the sick whose injured organs he touches and salves with saliva, to the lepers he holds, to the children he embraces. All the people—and the disciples in particular—had become so accustomed to this highly concrete and challenging presence that Jesus' farewell, departure and absence were bound to be felt as a very deliberate act, both on his part and on theirs. When he told them of it, they did not understand and, initially, were bound to misinterpret it. "Where does this man intend to go that we shall not find him? Does he intend to go to the Dispersion among the Greeks and teach the Greeks?" (Jn 7:35). Or, "Will he kill himself, since he says, 'Where I am going, you cannot come'?" (Jn 8:22). The apostles too hear him announce his departure but, thinking in terms of earthly presence, fail to

125

understand. They either naively profess that they want to die with him (that is, refusing to allow the intended separation to take place), like Thomas (Jn 11:16) and Peter (Mk 14:31; Mt 26:35; Lk 22:33); or they insist that they want to stay with him at all costs (Mt 26:33), no doubt imagining that they could defend him and prevent him from dying (Mk 8:32); or else they ask which way he is going, so that they can go with him (Peter: Jn 13:36; Thomas: Jn 14:5), or ask for an immediate revelation of his goal (Philip: Jn 14:8). For the present, however, the only answer is this: "Little children, yet a little while I am with you. You will seek me; and as I said to the Jews so now I say to you, 'Where I am going you cannot come'" (Jn 13:33 = 7:34 = 8:21). Nor is this invalidated when the resurrected Lord appears to the disciples on earth. The gap between heaven and earth remains and is stressed explicitly in the fact that they do not recognize him. He appears in "another form" (Lk 24:16; Mk 16:12; Jn 20:11; 21:5), which is only briefly transformed into a form familiar to them. As soon as he is recognized (Lk 24:31; Jn 20:17), the form disappears, leaving behind a vocation to be exercised in the Church.

Essentially, the particular "local" references in Luke's account of the Ascension simply underline the definitive nature of this inner "distance", in the appearances of the Risen One, between him and his disciples. These appearances schooled the Church in the proper attitude of faith, yet it was still necessary for the angel to deliver a special admonition to the disciples as they kept looking wistfully after the ascended Jesus; they had to be reminded of their earthly vocation and that they would see him again at the end of time (Acts 1:11). The experience of Jesus' presence is only the means and the point of departure, setting the believing Church on its path through time, a path of unforeseeable duration and (viewed from the outside) of loneliness. The last logion of the first conclusion of John's Gospel sums it up: "Blessed are those who have not seen and yet believe" (Jn 20:29).

This ultimate faith relationship is obscure to the senses, so much so that even in the inner circle "some doubted" (Mt 28:17), and in the wider circle people said that the body had been stolen (Mt 28:13), and improbable rumors circulated concerning "one Jesus, who was dead, but whom Paul asserted to be alive" (Acts 25:19). Obscure though it is, this relationship had to be practiced and cultivated throughout Jesus' entire earthly life. It is a life full of farewells, separations, withdrawals, both external and internal. Not only is there the official attempt to eliminate Jesus' very existence right at the outset as something unwelcome (Mt 2:16)—wherever his presence is openly proclaimed he is essentially unrecognized: "Among you stands one whom you do not know" (Jn 1:26)— and whom John himself did not recognize until he received the sign (1:30ff.). On the one hand, he cannot "trust himself to them" (2:24), and on the other hand, when he does disclose himself, he is "not received" and hence "not known" (1:11, 10). This element of otherness right at the heart of his presence causes him to seem absent even when he is present: he went up to the feast "not publicly but in private". "The Jews were looking for him at the feast, and saying, 'Where is he?' " (Jn 7:10). Communication fails because he wants to give himself in a way people do not expect. His presence, which seems impossible, is wrapped in mystery and appears like absence. Similarly, the disciples' faith is insufficient to recognize him as he walks toward them on the water at night: they cry out with terror, for "they thought it was a ghost" (Mk 6:49). It is a continuing problem: "Have I been with you so long, and yet you do not know me?" (Jn 14:9). The "distance" created by unbelief, smallness of faith or fear (Jn 21:12) is a prelude to the Passion, where it is not primarily Jesus who leaves his own, but he who is forsaken by them: "The hour is coming, indeed it has come, when you will be scattered, every man to his home, and will leave me alone" (Jn 16:32). "Then all the disciples forsook him and fled" (Mt 26:56). Even before the Passion, it is the fact that Jesus is not inwardly accepted that causes him to keep an external distance and be absent. Thus in Nazareth, where they want to "throw him down headlong. But passing through the midst of them he went away" (Lk 4:30). So too, in the last days prior to his suffering, when he "no longer went about openly among the Jews, but went from there to the country near the wilderness" (Jn 11:54). Mark puts this process of distancing quite early on: the disciples run to find Jesus, who has disappeared; they find him praying and tell him, "Everyone is searching for you." The answer comes, "Let us go on to the next towns. . . ." (Mk 1:35ff.). For he is essentially the wanderer, the one who withdraws: "I must go on my way today and tomorrow and the day following" (Lk 13:33). The same withdrawal becomes

128

necessary when the Jews misunderstand his miracle of the loaves and want to make him a king: "Jesus withdrew again to the hills by himself" (Jn 6:15). Here, too, belong the practically countless "crossings" to the "other shore", which are almost always instances of distancing. And all this takes place in the midst of a public life that, far from having periods of contemplation built into it, finds Jesus ceaselessly among men, preaching and working miracles.

Though people fail to recognize it and profit from it, his presence is, as such, God's promised time of salvation, yet it is only a "little while". It is a time that still lasts, yet, as it were, is beginning to pass away. " 'The light is with you for a little longer. Walk while you have the light, lest the darkness overtake you. . . .' When Jesus had said this, he departed and hid himself from them" (Jn 12:35f.). "As long as I am in the world, I am the light of the world" (9:5). In Jn 16:16 the "little while" becomes a kind of hidden key to Jesus' whole manner of earthly existence and suffering. Two things interpenetrate in this key word: the economy of grace given from above, which allows the invisible to appear visible for a little while, and the contrary economy of sin, which does not want to see what has been manifested, banishing it into invisibility and absence.

Both aspects are inextricably interrelated when Jesus himself arranges his absences, for both of them provide a single motivation for his absence with its significance for salvation. These deliberate absences are especially clear when Jesus chooses particular disciples to experience certain manifestations of his presence. Thus only Peter, John and James are taken into the house of

Jairus to see the raising of his daughter; they alone are taken up to the Mountain of the Transfiguration to glimpse the other worldly figure of Jesus, and, correspondingly, they alone are permitted to be close to Jesus on the Mount of Olives when he wrestles with the Father's will. So too in the Church there are individuals, elected ones, recipients of special grace, who experience the modes of Jesus' presence, where others—expressly and deliberately the majority—are set at a distance and feel him to be absent from their senses. On the Mount of Olives, the places are allotted with precise gradations. The traitor lurks at an infinite remove, eight disciples are told: "Sit here, while I pray" (Mk 14:32), and the three chosen ones are taken further and then told to "remain here, and watch" (14:3). He himself goes "a little farther", "about a stone's throw" (Lk 22:41). Here we have a "hierarchy of absences"—it is a permanent feature in the Church. No one has a right to a particular experience of the Lord's nearness, but it means a great deal if a person accepts the particular mode of nearness the Lord offers him and abides in it, watching and praying, instead of sleeping and falling into a culpable absence.

We are initiated further into the mystery of Jesus' saving absence by the strange events involving the women close to him. The life of his mother, Mary, is totally under the sign of the piercing sword (Lk 2:35), which is essentially a sword of separation as well. The aspect of separation comes into view at Cana: "Woman, what have you to do with me?" (Jn 2:4) and is intensified in the scene in which Jesus refuses her visit: "Who are my mother and my brothers?" (Mk 3:33). It comes to fulfillment on the Cross, when the Son withdraws from his mother and foists another son on her: "Woman, behold, your son!" (Jn 19:26)—thus introducing her into the same God-forsakenness that he himself is experiencing at the Father's hand. For the degree of closeness to Jesus' destiny and mission is the degree of participation in his central soteriological experience. At this point, the measure of inner fellowship with Jesus is the measure of our experience of absence.

The destiny of the mother, Mary, is reported only in a few key words, but the same reality is indicated at greater length in the story of the women of Bethany left desolate by the death of their brother. Once again, the whole scene is set with unmistakable deliberateness. The sisters are above in Bethany; Jesus is below by the Jordan. He receives an urgent message to come immediately but deliberately delays: "Jesus loved Martha and her sister and Lazarus. So when he heard that he was ill, he stayed two days longer in the place where he was. Then after this he said to the disciples, 'Let us go into Judea again. . . . Are there not twelve hours in the day? . . . I am glad that I was not there, so that you may believe'" (Jn 11:6–15). By the time he arrives Lazarus is dead, but that is not the worst: rather, it is the fact that he left the sisters without any word, in the dark night of God's absence. "If you had been here", says Martha, as she rushes to meet him (11:21). "Lord, if you had been here", says Mary at his feet (11:32). We are twice told that Jesus was "deeply moved" and wept (11:33, 35, 38). It was hardly at Lazarus' physical death that he wept, for we read

nothing of the kind at the raising of the dead elsewhere. Rather, he must have been deeply moved at the
inner tragic dimension in which he had to share his
God-forsakenness on the Cross (eucharistically and by
way of anticipation) with those he loved in a special
way. Needless to say, what we are speaking of here are
utterly personal destinies, allotted by grace ("mystical"), not some diffuse and vague sentiment of our age
to the effect that "God is dead." The latter experience
is much more complex and impure than the former,
which has a sharp outline and is explicitly imparted to
those who love Jesus. Only they, on the basis of their
experience of his presence, can genuinely suffer its
negative side, his absence.

Such was the experience of the third Mary, the former sinner of Magdala, on Easter morning, when she
went weeping to the empty tomb to look for the
vanished dead man. Even the appearance of angels
could not console her in the face of this void, nor even
the presence of Jesus under a different guise. It was as if
her entire being were concentrated in a single act of
searching. "If you have carried him away, tell me
where you have laid him, and I will take him away" (Jn
20:15). She was so deeply bereft because she had stood
beneath the Cross and had realized there what it had
really cost the beloved Lord to drive out her seven
devils. She has lost herself entirely as a result of this
experience; she "lives no longer" except "by faith in
the Son of God, who loved me and gave himself for
me" (Gal 2:20). In her case, this living "out of oneself"
and "in the beloved" is a living for, in and toward a
dead man. Her excess of love is ultimate. The experi-

ence of Easter—"Mary!" "Rabbouni!"—only transforms it. *Noli me tangere:* the sudden presence of the Living One is not there to be grasped and held but to be let go; she is given just as much sense experience as she needs so that the Lord, withdrawing from her and going to the Father, can send her as a messenger to the brethren. The spark of experienced presence suffices to transform empty absence into an absence that is brimful.

Jesus' existential form is that of appearing in vanishing, of self-giving while eluding every attempt to hold him. And this very form shows him to be not only the image and likeness but the definitive Word of the God "who dwells in unapproachable light, whom no man has ever seen or can see" (1 Tim 6:16), and yet whose grace "has appeared for the salvation of all men" (Titus 2:11). So the Lord never withdraws from the person who seeks him and is turned toward him without having imparted to him the blessing and grace of his presence. The many people he bids "Go"—"go and sin no more", "go and show yourself . . .", "go and declare how much God has done for you" and so on—carry his presence with them into their lives henceforth, lives to which Jesus returns them. Indeed, sometimes he expressly sends them back to live at a distance that makes a closer discipleship impossible (Lk 8:38). As for the special discipleship, the way of the Twelve is (like the way of the Marys) a continual school of letting go of direct contact and possession. Thus, we can say that the counsel of "leaving everything", even where it is not an explicit command, indicates the path of discipleship in a very concentrated and mysterious sense: the Christian too, together with Jesus, is "absent", from the world's point of view, so that he may be present to it in a more concentrated yet incomprehensible way on the basis of a divine commission. The Christian's mission in the world presupposes that he has died to the world, not only in following the earthly path of Jesus but also so that he may become the place where the absolutely elusive dialectic of God's ever-greater immanence in ever-greater transcendence shall be permanently displayed.

However mankind's religions and Christian theologies may adumbrate their pictures of God—in inexhaustible plurality—none of them can claim to be a genuine approximation to the mystery unless it submits to Augustine's phrase, which is valid for time and eternity: *Si comprehendis non est Deus*—"If you think you have grasped it, it is not God."

4. Office and existence

Anyone in office has the power to exercise authority, to issue orders, for the good of the community. In a democracy, the office of leadership is subject to the scrutiny of those who obey: they have elected the office-bearers and equipped them with their powers, and consequently they can judge how far the exercise of office furthers the common good. This is critical obedience, going no further than the insight of those who obey. This model cannot apply to the constitution of the people of God of the Old and New Testaments, for it is not democratic but theocratic and Christo-cratic. Here power is not granted by the people, but by God and Christ. This applies to the entire biblical realm. While we are limiting ourselves in this study to portraying the biblical realm, our intention is to use this to shed light on two contemporary issues. First: Can there be a Christian exercise of office where the latter is not backed up by the life of the office-bearer? Second: Can those who obey apply criticism to the office-bearers even if the latter do not draw their power from them?

1. In the total context of the Bible

All the chief actors in Old and New Testament history are characterized by a unity of their mission and their life. Their mission always comes from God; the man to whom it is granted is always required to commit his whole life to his mission. The act by which he offers himself for this service, whether it is described as faith, commitment, obedience, docility or whatever, expropriates him even in his most intimate personal sphere for the benefit of his service, which is always a service to the people of God. Thus expropriated, the commissioned servant accepts responsibility for his task in an unlimited obedience. From Moses we can see that the slightest disobedience or unbelief toward God is severely punished, because his grave responsibility for the distressed and quarreling people cannot for a moment be based on his private ideas: it must always be an expression of the will of God. This can be the case only if the commissioned servant stays in vital communication, through prayerful obedience, with his divine commissioner.

Abraham has this kind of communication with God. He believes God's promise which refers to his future descendants. His whole existence hangs on it, going to the ultimate of blind obedience by being prepared to sacrifice his own son for the sake of the promise without "critically" accusing God of contradiction. In the course of Moses' call, his stubborn clinging to his own ideas has to be broken by God; otherwise, he could have been neither the mediator between God and the people nor a wise leader of the people. Yahweh appoints Joshua, the righteous man "in whom is the spirit", to be Moses' successor by the laying on of hands (Nb 27:18), and Yahweh himself instructs Joshua: "You shall meditate on [the book of the law] day and night, that you may be careful to do according to all that is written in it" (Jos 1:8). It is Yahweh, again, who "raised up judges", "was with them" and suddenly overtook them with his Spirit (Jg 2:16, 18; 3:10 etc.). As the nation's social structures stabilize, it is Yahweh who chooses the king and, when his obedience proves imperfect, rejects him and replaces him with another ("I have provided for myself a king": 1 Sam 16:1). And when God guarantees the dynasty that begins with David, he makes the proviso that, if any successor separates office from obedience, he will "chasten him with the rods of men, with the stripes of the sons of men" (2 Sam 7:14). The institution of the priestly office is based on an analogous total consecration of life (Levi opts for Yahweh: Dt 33:8ff.; Yahweh takes the Levites instead of the firstborn, so that they henceforth belong to him: Nb 3:12ff.; they forfeit their share in the land: "Yahweh is their inheritance": Jos 13:33).[1] The origins of prophesy lie hidden

---

[1] At all points we are viewing the history of Israel as it has been formulated on the basis of its own theological self-understanding. This picture is normative and is the only one which concerns us.

in the mists of time, yet it seems that, from the beginning, prophesy was a way of life (cf. 1 Sam 19:20). Elijah, for instance, was totally absorbed by his prophetic mission, and in the great figures of prophetic literature, the claim of the word of God penetrates more and more deeply into the prophet's personal life (for example, Jeremiah, Ezekiel). Eventually we meet the picture of the ideal hearer of the word (Is 50:4), who not only genuinely *performs* the word but perfectly *suffers* it—foreshadowing the coming Redeemer.

The Redeemer, Jesus Christ, unites office and existence totally. In him the commission is personified: he is the Word of the Father as his Son, and the Son of the Father as his Word. All thought of the two being in any way unconnected is excluded with increasing firmness in the New Testament writers' reflection on his being and destiny. He is the Word-made-flesh; he knows it and presents himself as such. This comes to a climax in the paradox that, in his suffering on behalf of men, he is both priest and victim, both the officially appointed executant and the existential sufferer of ultimate woe (forsakenness by God). If there is to be official authority in his Church—and he gave such authority with the greatest possible explicitness (Mk 3:15, 6:7; Mt 10:1, 16:19; Lk 9:19; Jn 21:15ff.)—it can only be in the most intimate connection with a form of life that calls for total availability for the mission (Mt 8:18ff., etc.) and that, moreover, involves a promise: the highest representative of Church office is promised death on the Cross (Jn 21:19), and, in Jesus' high-priestly prayer, the apostles present are "consecrated in truth"

in the same sacrificial consecration of life as Jesus himself (Jn 17:17, 19). Seen in the context of the official
priest of the New Covenant, Jesus Christ, such participation in his priest-victim identity on the part of
church officers who come after him is not something
optional, accidental and excessive. On the contrary, it
is the stigma characterizing New Testament office.
Later heretics, such as the Montanists and Donatists,
occasionally sensed this quite correctly, even if they
drew the false conclusion that a Christian priest who
does not live out the holiness that attaches to his office
is unable to mediate the grace of Christ to the people of
God. All would agree that such a case is grotesque, an
impossible possibility, theologically speaking. Yet,
grotesque as it is, it has not the power to destroy the
work of Christ and the life of his Church. The life and
writings of Paul seal the possibility of bringing official
authority and life into a harmony in Christian discipleship, and Paul remains the model for all subsequent
office in the Church. Timothy took him as his example: "You have observed my teaching, my conduct, my
aim in life, my faith, my patience, my love, my steadfastness, my persecutions, my sufferings" (2 Tim
3:10f.). Paul is always using his life as an argument, as a
demonstration of the teaching he proclaims, even
though in doing so he never equates himself with
Christ; he is only an "ambassador for Christ" (2 Cor
5:19), yet also his "fellow worker" (this is how he also
describes the other official holders of authority: Rom
16:21; 1 Cor 3:9, 16:16; 2 Cor 8:23; Phil 2:25, 4:3). On
the basis of the grace of his calling, and in his self-

surrender in faith, he participates in that identity of office and existence that are found in Christ and are communicated by him.

2. Identity in Christ

So far, we have seen the continuity from Abraham and Moses to Paul: in the realm of the Bible, God imparts no significant office unless the office-bearer puts his whole existence at God's disposal. But this ubiquitous fundamental law is rendered more acute in the transition from the Old to the New Covenant, for Israel was a "fleshly" people, whereas the Church is the "spiritual Israel". Old Israel was still subject to sociological determinisms, but these have vanished with the coming of Jesus. The Letter to the Hebrews sharply and almost one-sidedly[2] stresses the hiatus: the institutional priesthood of the Old Covenant has been abolished in the unique, once-for-all existential priesthood of Christ. Essential though this affirmation is, it is not intended to deny either that there was an interpenetration of office and existence even in the Old Covenant, or that there are to be such living embodiments of office in the New. It simply puts an end to the national, impersonal institution—just as the dynastic priesthood and kingship had come to an end. Among ancient peoples, the king was regarded as inspired purely on the basis of his

[2] For the correctives to be discerned in Hebrews itself and in the rest of the New Testament cf. Heribert Mühlen *Entsakralisierung* (Schöningh, 1971) 283ff; also International Theological Commission: *Priesterdienst* (Einsiedeln: Johannes Verlag, 1972).

office; in Israel the priest possessed a certain prophetic charism in declaring the word of God purely on the basis of his inherited role, but the prophets already sharply criticized this, as it were, "natural" element and particularly its abuse. Jeremiah had scornfully confronted the politicking "peace priests" and "peace prophets" who were not authorized by Yahweh (6:14, 8:11, 23:17 etc.); in the postexilic Ps 85 we can still hear this kind of "cultic prophet" uttering his "priestly oracle of salvation". It was the magical and automatic side of the old cult, which seemed to dispense those involved from existential faith—quite apart from the toleration of idolatry in the Temple—that the prophets attacked. And Jesus himself, who prayed and worshipped in the Temple and sent those he had healed to show themselves to the priests, and even taught that people should respect the *"cathedra"* of the Pharisees and Scribes, does not criticize the existing office and its authority as such but rather its abuse. He knows that only he himself can bring about perfect identity between office and existence, and that all previous attempts are only valid insofar as they anticipate him (Lk 24:25ff.; Jn 5:46, 8:56). If the Letter to the Hebrews stresses the hiatus between what was formerly "mere" institution and what is now its fulfillment in Christ's personal obedience, the theme of the Shepherd that Jesus draws from the Old Covenant and applies to himself demonstrates, conversely, the unbroken continuity.[3]

[3] On the theme of the Shepherd cf. the bibliography in Joachim Jeremias's article *Poimèn* in *ThWNT* (1959); Odo Kiefer, *Die Hirtenrede, Stuttgarter Bibl. Stud.* 23 (1967); A. J. Simonis, "Die Hir-

God is the Shepherd of Israel (Ps 23): in this image authority and life are perfectly identical at their source. On this basis God could appoint "shepherds" in Israel to represent him—Moses and David were genuine shepherds[4]—shepherds who were to pasture the flock by his commission and in his spirit. And when the shepherds start "feeding themselves" instead of the flock, and the sheep get lost in the mountains, God promises (Ezek 34) to step in himself and look after them: he will "seek the lost . . . bring back the strayed . . . bind up the crippled . . . strengthen the weak" (34:16) and separate the sheep from the goats and so forth. And in order to do this he will "set over them one shepherd, my servant David" (34:23), so that "they shall all have one shepherd" (37:24). In the synoptic parable, Jesus portrays this divine Shepherd, who (in him) goes to look for the lost sheep and brings it home. In the Johannine picture of the Shepherd, he shows that he himself is this divine Shepherd, commissioned and empowered by the Father, who goes to the lengths of giving his life for his sheep—in sharp contrast to the hirelings, who, while they exercise an office of a kind over the flock, draw back from total commitment (Jn 10). The image of a shepherd who proves his "Chief Shepherd's" (1 Pet 5:4) authority by

tenrede im Johannesevangelium" *Analecta Biblica* 29 (Rome: Pontifical Biblical Institute, 1967); I. de la Potterie, "Le Bon Pasteur" *Communio* 11 (Rome, 1969).

[4] Cf. Dominique Barthélémy, "Zwei Hirten als Entdecker Gottes" in *Gott mit seinem Ebenbild. Umrisse einer biblischen Theologie* (German translation: [Einsiedeln: Johannes Verlag, 1966]) 133ff.

dying for the flock (and thus apparently leaving them in the lurch) is just as paradoxical as the image of the high priest in Hebrews, who appears before God alive, bearing "his own [shed] blood". Fundamentally, it is the same image and the same paradox, since in both cases absolute authority is the consequence of absolute personal involvement: Jesus is the "good (that is, genuine) Shepherd" and simultaneously the "great" High Priest (Heb 4:14). It is a further instance of the paradox according to which Jesus has authority to raise to life on the Last Day those who eat his flesh and drink his blood, that is, those who associate themselves with his destruction in death—a death from which he can emerge as the "life of the world" (Jn 6). From an earthly point of view this kind of authority, given by the Father, seems close to madness—to suicide (Jn 8:22)—since it is the power freely to "lay down" his own life (Jn 10:18). We can only get beyond this insanity if we recognize the *identity of authority and mission* in Jesus. The mission is so much a personified one that ultimately it is the Father who performs the act of surrender (Jn 3:16; Rom 8:32); ultimately, it is simply the utter freedom of the Father's saving action that is revealed in the Son's free consent.

At this point everything has become personal, the last vestige of national or earthly institution has vanished. Now, when Jesus imparts the Old Testament pastoral authority and charge—which he has perfected—to Peter and his "fellow elders", it is still concerned with the same thing, namely, representing God, his authority and his deeds, but now it is stamped by the personal involvement of Christ and is accompanied by an allotted portion of his unlimited authority (Mt 28:18f.). In the Old Covenant, as in the whole of the Near East, the image of the shepherd initially referred to the king (not to the priest insofar as he was distinct from the king, nor to the prophet); it denoted the king who was conscious of his task, conscientious and "good". Hence the attribute was applied to Yahweh with its irreversible sequence of authority—commitment. Even the earliest part of the Ethiopic Book of Enoch (prior to 160 B.C.) describes the history of Israel as that of a flock of lambs with the *Kyrios* as their shepherd. Here Moses, Samuel and David are also referred to as "sheep". The shepherd embodies divine authority, but he always embodies Yahweh's self-involvement on Israel's behalf as well (chap. 88–90).[5]

In the New Testament, this authority passes exclusively to the person of the Son and every other religious authority has to yield to his; when the Son confers authority he does so on an exclusively personal basis. In Christian terms, according to the Son's manner of life—the Son is invested with the Father's authority as one who is "obedient unto death"—such authority is only given to those who bring to it the total offering of their lives ("Simon, do you love me more than these?") and who manifest a readiness that goes beyond their own will ("Another will gird you and carry you where you do not wish to go"). In his Magna Carta for the clergy, Peter hands on what he has received: authority is to be exercised "not by con-

[5] Cf. A. J. Simonis (note 3 above), 161–168: Enoch as the background for Jn 10.

straint but willingly" and "not for shameful gain but eagerly, not as domineering over those in your charge but being examples to the flock" (1 Pet 5:2f.). The term that is always recurring in Paul for leadership of the community (his own and that of his colleagues) is *kopiān,* "to toil", "to exhaust oneself": it is precisely because Christians have this clear witness before their eyes that they should "be subject" (1 Cor 16:16) and "respect" those set over them (1 Th 5:12), not refusing them the fruits of their labors (2 Tim 2:6). Similarly, Heb 13:7 sees authority and the testimony of a life in a single unity: "Remember your leaders, those who spoke to you the word of God"—authority and proclamation of the word are viewed as one—"Consider the outcome of their life, and imitate their faith."

3. Obedience and criticism in the Church

We began by saying that authority in the Church can only be understood theocratically and Christo-cratically, not democratically. This has a built-in safety proviso: Christ has authority *insofar as* he is obedient to the Father unto death and in this obedience becomes the servant of all. We can see how this translates in terms of the Church in Paul, who understands himself as a "servant and steward of the mysteries of God". "It is required of stewards that they be found trustworthy. . . . It is the Lord who judges me." He is not prepared to give an account to the community or any other human court and warns the community against judging him "before the time"—of God's judgment—

(1 Cor 4:1–5). On the other hand, however, he lays his manner of life open before the community so that they themselves can compare his official activity with his life. Such comparison is legitimate. The Corinthians are also invited to compare their own conduct with what they believe. The results turn out to the advantage of the apostle and the disadvantage of the community: for "We are fools for Christ's sake, but you are wise in Christ; we are weak, but you are strong. You are held in honour, but we in disrepute. . . . Already you are filled! Already you have become rich! Without us you have become kings!" (1 Cor 4:10, 8). And this contrast has a theological explanation: "So death is at work in us, but life in you" (2 Cor 4:12): the apostle's closeness to the sufferings of Christ merits nearness to the Resurrection on behalf of the community. But the contrast can also be seen as a great danger: you democratic Christians who have come of age think that you are already living on the other side of the Cross in an imaginary Resurrection; we office-bearers, humiliated, stand under the Cross. But since the Cross is and remains the only, perpetual way of access to the risen life, Paul begins his school of faith again at chapter one: "lest the Cross of Christ be emptied of its power", he determines "to know nothing among you"—in Corinth—"except Jesus Christ and him crucified" (1 Cor 1:17, 2:2).

But have not the people of God the right to discern this unity of authority and life in its leaders and hence to arrive at a critical assessment as to whether and how far this unity can be ascertained? Have they not received the prerequisite for such an assessment, namely, the Spirit of God in the charisms that God himself has given them? Does not the image of the shepherd and the sheep fail at this point insofar as it seems to reserve all authority to the shepherd and all obedience to the flock—a view that has been transcended since Christ's obedience unto death? At this point, Paul steps in to dissolve the apparently confused and hopelessly tangled dialectic of obedience and criticism in the Church. Criticism is by no means rejected a priori as inappropriate, but it has a substantial precondition, that is, that the critics examine themselves "to see whether you are holding to your faith": "Are you aware that Jesus Christ is in you?" (2 Cor 13:5)—namely, the Jesus Christ whose mysterious obedience unto death is and remains the precondition for his risen, pneumatic existence. If the critics are not prepared to undergo this test, they will be judged to have failed it. This would show that they were not standing at the center of Christian existence, which is the only vantage point from which the Christian life of an office-bearer can be assessed. However, Paul hopes that "you will find out that *we* have not failed." Why not? Because his whole life has been fashioned according to Christ's life and mode of authority: "For he was crucified in weakness, but lives by the power of God. For we are weak in him, but in dealing with you we shall live with him by the power of God" (13:4). So he is hopeful that the Corinthians will come to understand the paradox of authority in the Church by experiencing in faith the mystery of Christ ("when I am weak, then I am strong": 12:10). Once again he is ready to let them have the glamor of seeming mature while he accepts humili-

147

ation on their behalf: "We pray to God that you may not do wrong—not that *we* may appear to have met the test, but that *you* may do what is right, though *we* may seem to have failed. . . . For we are glad when we are weak and you are strong." For the whole authority of the New Testament office-bearer only has meaning in the context of building up the community. Here again we see the contrast between "fleshly" authority in the Old Covenant and "spiritual" authority in the New. Whereas Jeremiah is given power "to pluck up and to break down, to destroy and to overthrow, to build and to plant" (Jer 1:10), Paul, evidently with this in mind, says: "I write this while I am away from you, in order that when I come I may not have to be severe in my use of the authority which the Lord has given me for building up and *not* for tearing down" (2 Cor 13:10).

True, he had previously said that "the weapons of our warfare are not worldly but have divine power to destroy strongholds. We destroy arguments and every proud obstacle to the knowledge of God" (2 Cor 10:4f.). But it transpires that he only wants to use this power with the consent and understanding of the believing community. So it is in the case of the man excommunicated for incest: Paul has already decided the issue as far as he himself is concerned but wants to implement his decision together with the community assembled around him in the Spirit (1 Cor 6:3ff.). And he is "ready to punish every disobedience, when your obedience is complete", so that the latter can approve the punishment (2 Cor 10:6). He can threaten with "naked" authority if the community is in danger of severing itself, through its criticism of authority, from the Church's fellowship of obedience in faith and love. But as a man of the Church he sees such a situation as a fundamentally impossible exception, a fiasco: it would indicate the destruction of the *communio,* whose inner form, according to Paul, is due in considerable measure to office, lived and exercised in a Christlike manner. "For I fear that perhaps *I* may come and find *you* not what *I* wish, and that *you* may find *me* not what *you* wish; that perhaps there may be quarreling, jealousy, anger, selfishness, slander, gossip, conceit and disorder. I fear that when I come again my God may humble me before you. . . . If I come again I will not spare them—since you desire proof that Christ is speaking in me" (2 Cor 12:20f.; 13:2f.). If they were looking for "proof" in an attitude of "tempting God" and of deliberate dispute (= Massah and Meribah: Ex 17:7), such proof could not be given by authority in the way envisaged in the Church. Instead, it would have to be given in the veiled form of humiliation, that is, naked power. But in that case the community itself would be to blame for having failed the test.

This does not mean that the community has no critical function to perform vis-à-vis authority. The leaders of the communities are to form all the members of the Church so that they can exercise their particular ministry; they are to lead them out of a condition of immaturity in both faith and life and educate them to "speak the truth in love" (Eph 4:12ff.). Since all the members are to be "knit together" in mutual service as a result of this training in responsible action, there certainly is an interplay between Christians and their leaders. Paul himself is always wanting to be edified, consoled, accompanied spiritually and encouraged by the communities. There is an interplay of *"paraklesis"*—both consolation and admonishment—back and forth between all members of the body of Christ. Thus each member of the community is encouraged to make a positive contribution toward building up the whole, and such contribution may and must be a critical one. Even in the Pastoral Letters (1 Tim 5:20f.), it is envisaged that priests may fail, that complaints may arise against them from the community and that they may have to be reprimanded by the bishop "in the presence of all", albeit "without favor and . . . partiality". Here the leader is to be, among other things, "gentle" (3:3). But there is a standard below which he must not fall: he is always presupposed to be "without fault", "an example in speech and conduct, in love, in faith, in purity" (1 Tim 4:12)—just as Paul understood himself as an example *(typos)* who in turn bore the stamp of Christ. Under this proviso, Paul confirms his successor in a kind of holy imperturbability that, while from the outside it can look like rigidity, inwardly is nothing other than the office-bearer's obedience and responsibility toward his Lord.

We do not need to follow all the meanderings in which Paul defends himself against the community. Nor do we need to represent his self-defense as the concrete, detailed model for later debates within the Church. What is essential in it (extending through many chapters of a major Pauline epistle) is that it is an example of dialogue between office in the Church and a community critical of it. It would be a mistake to say that this dialogue is only of historical interest since in later times no bishop or priest can aspire to the same authority as that of an apostle. The New Testament does not contain antiquities of that kind. The practical Church teaching of the two Letters to the Corinthians has the same scope of application as the soteriology of Romans and Galatians. Protestant theology ought to have taken it just as seriously as it took the latter. For it translates the doctrine of salvation into the terms of the present-day Church, a Church that still possesses the fundamental structure with which it appeared in apostolic times.

Paul uses his life as an argument, for it is essentially congruent with his office, yet he is proud of it only insofar as, by God's grace, it has been modeled on the Lord's life. Not many of the later Church's office-bearers will be able to follow him in this kind of exhibition of his life ("foolishness"), nor will they want to. But they will all have the example of Paul in their mind's eye, particularly in his desire to use naked authority only in exceptional cases and in his efforts to do everything to avert them, overcoming the hiatus between office and community by the "mind of Christ", and not least in the way Paul makes the judgmental and critical community think again about its criticism of the weakness of those in office.

5. Joy and the Cross

I

The very word "gospel", *"eu-angelion"*, shows that Christianity is "glad tidings" and that its whole tenor must be indisputably that of joy. It is "good news of a great joy" and "peace on earth" (Lk 2:10, 14), and peace and joy are often interchangeable terms for the ultimate blessing of salvation (Jn 14:27, 16:33; Rom 14:17; Gal 5:22). Thus it is a heightening of the Old Testament joy of the believer in God in his revealed word,[1] a heightening of the religious cultic joy of Israel[2]—and we know with what joy Jews celebrate their feasts to this day!—because the "Word" becomes "flesh" and, through his Crucifixion, God's love for us acquires a

[1] J. Nielen, "Die Freude am Wort und an der Weisung Gottes im Licht der Psalmen" in *Leben aus dem Wort* (Patmos 1962) 36–51.

[2] Bo Reicke, *Diakonie, Festfreude und Zelos* (Uppsala, 1951). P. Humbert, "'Laetari et exultare' dans le vocabulaire religieux de l'Ancien Testament" *RHPhR* 22 (1942): 185–214. Id., *Opuscules d'un Hébraisant* (Neuchâtel, 1958), 119–145.

152

perfect, unsurpassable expression (Rom 8:32ff.). So New Testament joy is not to be queried, restricted or relativized by any other attitude. It is not only a response to the attitude in heaven, where every tear will be wiped away (Rev 7:17, 21:4), but a response to the ultimate attitude of God himself, whose "greater joy" is manifest in pardoning sin and in finding what was lost and gone astray (Lk 15:7, 10;[3] cf. vv. 24, 32). This passage speaks of the joy of God as Father, and consequently this joy must be manifest in the Son who reveals him; indeed, he "rejoices" at the way the Father reveals himself (Lk 10:21; cf. Rev 2:26, 28). And just as Jesus "rejoiced in the Holy Spirit", the joy of believers, if it is to be a proper response to God's joy, can only come about in the Holy Spirit. It is the Spirit who brings about joy (an eschatologcal joy, the harbinger of heaven), even as early as the infancy narrative (Lk 1:14, 44–47) and then fully blown after the Lord's Resurrection (Acts 13:52; cf. 5:41). Insofar as this Christian joy has an eternally transcendent object, that is, the revelation of the love of God that does not cling to itself, it also manifests a subjectively transcendent quality, which is why John will describe it five times as "full" or "complete" joy (15:11, 16:24, 17:13; 1 Jn 1:4; 2 Jn 12). This sense of being totally filled means that we have been brought to eschatological perfection.[4]

However, this renders the problem of joy and the Cross all the more difficult. From what we have already said it is inevitable that we should understand all

[3] In these passages the expressions "heaven" and "angel of God" are reverent circumlocutions for God himself.

[4] Bultmann, *The Gospel of John* (Oxford 1971).

suffering in God's definitive, New Testament revelation (both in Christ and in the Christian) as being only
a function of joy—and seek to justify it as such. But by
doing this we could be breaking off suffering's ultimate, most painful tip in the way it is deliberately and
consciously broken off in Buddhism or Stoicism, for
instance, by the notion of *apatheia*. This would mean
that suffering would not really be taken seriously in
Christianity. If, then, this unacceptable conclusion is to
be rejected and Christ's Cross is to be allowed the
absolute seriousness of God-forsakenness—which is
essential if Christ was "made to be sin" and "made a
curse" for us (2 Cor 5:21; Gal 3:13; cf. Rom 8:3) and
"was given up for our sake";[5] and if, moreover, the
disciple's "following" of Jesus to the Cross (Jn 21:19)
must at least bring him to the point where the suffering of the Cross is taken seriously as a criterion, how
can we still speak of joy?

One could attempt to solve the dilemma from two
angles. First, Jesus' suffering on the Cross, including
his being forsaken by God, could be seen as a paradoxical expression of his joy. Albert Frank-Duquesne
("Joie de Jésus-Christ")[6] once made a very serious at-

[5] Wiard Popkes, *Christus traditus. Eine Untersuchung zum Begriff der
Dahingabe im Neuen Testament* (Zwingliverlag 1967).

[6] In "Ma Joie terrestre où donc es-tu?", *Études Carmélitaines*
(1947), 23–37. Some words of little Thérèse illustrate what Frank-
Duquesne means: "If you only knew how great my joy is to experience no joy in order to give joy to the Lord. It is so sublime a joy *(de
la joie raffinée)* although it is not experienced" (*Lettres*, 104). "I cannot
suffer any more, for all suffering has become sweet to me" (*Nov.
Verba*, 1926, 20f). "I have actually come to a place where I cannot
suffer any more, for all suffering has become sweet to me" (*Story of a*

tempt[7] to do this: "In spite of the desolation, the inconceivable, infernal forsakenness of his last hour on the Cross, no heart ever overflowed with such genuine joy as the heart of Jesus. . . . He is shaken with a hidden jubilation. It is as if the 'hell' of obscured love—beyond all enjoyment, at the point where self-reflection is no longer possible—actually constitutes the genuine, naked, unveiled reality of love and hence of joy . . . that magnificently bottomless, divinely free and spontaneous joy in obeying, the joy of loving to the point of sacrifice, the joy of self-surrender, a joy that is 'placed' entirely in God. . . . Here joy is no longer 'psychological' and experienced, and therefore somehow adventitious, contingent, accidental; it has acquired 'ontological' reality, grounding being itself, transcendent and divinizing."[8] We may already glimpse the answer to our question in these words, but it is premature: for can we really speak of joy where it is not experienced in any way?

Soul, 1947). "The path I am following has no consolation for me, and yet it contains all consolation" (*Lettres,* 165). "Although this trial robs me of every sensible pleasure, I can still cry out, 'Lord, you shower joy upon me in everything you do!' "(*Autobiographical Writings*).

[7] We are deliberately omitting discussion of the Scholastic theory according to which Jesus on the cross, because of the beatific vision which was always his, only suffered in the inferior powers of his soul. Thomas, *STh* III, q 46, a 7.

[8] Loc. cit. 24, 25, 31, 32. In his splendid little book on Claudel, Pierre Ganne takes a similar line: *Claudel. Humour, joie et liberté* (Éditions de l'Epi 1966). (German translation: *Die Freude ist die Wahrheit. Ein Gang durch das Werk Paul Claudels,* [Einsiedeln: Johannes Verlag, 1968]).

Let us approach the question from the other angle, that of the disciples: "Then they left the presence of the council, rejoicing that they were counted worthy to suffer dishonour for the name" (Acts 5:41). On this basis, we could attempt to interpret what Paul says about his being "crucified with Christ" (Gal 2:19) in close connection with the extreme physical and spiritual sufferings he enumerates: execration, persecution, slander, being regarded as the refuse of the world and the offscouring of all things (1 Cor 4:10–13); carrying in the body the death of Jesus (2 Cor 4:10); stigmata (however it is to be understood: Gal 6:17)— and we would have to put beside it this sentence, which is the hidden source of it all: "With all our affliction, I am overjoyed" (2 Cor 7:4). In the New Covenant, therefore, affliction and joy are often found together: Mt 5:13 par; Acts 7:55; 1 Th 1:6.

But have we actually got to the bottom of the question in these two attempts? Jesus says, "My soul is very sorrowful, even to death" (Mk 14:34; Mt 26:38). And what does Paul mean by saying that he "despaired of life itself" (2 Cor 1:8)? Do we not render the whole idea of suffering abstract and lifeless if we interpret it on the basis of joy? In fact, we have omitted something here, namely, the dimension of time, the succession of moments that must be filled with diverse and even contrary contents. "There is a time to weep, and a time to laugh; a time to mourn, and a time to dance . . ." (Qo 3:4). Now it will be said that neither Christ nor the Christian lose themselves in these contraries. There is a timeless vantage point, from which they survey them and assess their ultimate significance, namely, the

156

will of God, vocation. That is true. But surely the one who is "sent" is sent "away" from God on his particular mission; he must venture forth into the depths of the time dimension and, precisely as a Christian, must plumb its oppositions and contradictions. Does not the hymn to Christ in his obedience begin with the fact that he does not cling to his divine status but abandons it to the void of time (Phil 2:6–7)? The course set for Christ's mission points him to the destination of the Cross, which implies being forsaken by God and hence the loss of every joy, to "Death, with Hades at its heels" (Rev 6:8). At such a place all connection with joy—in God's sense and in the sense of the Kingdom of God—is utterly broken off (Ps 6:5 etc.). The person undergoing the "dark night" is totally incapable of connecting his experience with the joy that he has (forever!) lost.

So a second exploration is called for. We shall continue to take holy Scripture as our guide, but this time our method will not be a priori but a posteriori, following the path that starts from the entirely human experience of suffering and leads us step by step deeper into the Christian mystery. Then we shall see whether the Frank-Duquesne theory is substantiated or not.

2

Joy cannot be defined solely by reference to its object, since on the surface it is a condition and an affect of the subject.[9] On the other hand, however, it can be

[9] Thus we must disagree with E. G. Gulin who, in his *Die Freude im Neuen Testament* (2 vols, Helsinki 1932–1936) maintains that

equated even less with a state that might be described as a sense of physical well-being or even as a spiritual feeling of happiness. There can be no doubt that the word "blessed" in the Beatitudes refers to some joy, however hidden, but the subject, who is characterized as "poor", "mourning", "hungry and thirsty for righteousness", "persecuted" and "reviled", knows neither well-being nor happiness. The Beatitudes are not alone in the world's religious and philosophical literature; in fact, they are the highest instance of a universal human theme, namely, that at all levels, from the biological to the ethical, suffering and pain have a positive role. This is the case in the natural selection of the race as in the rearing of the individual, not only the rearing of the child by parent and school but in an ongoing way, by mature individuals. The latter only exist as such in the tension created by an ideal that is never completely realized, in going beyond themselves, in subjecting instinct to reason, inclination to duty, or, put less rigoristically, in the *"ethizesthai"* of the inclinations

---

(at least in John, cf. II, 67–71) joy is only spoken of with regard to its object. Further on the topic of Christian joy: Sarat, *La Joie dans S. Paul* (Lyons: Diss., 1931); W. Keppler, *Mehr Freude* (Freiburg, 1934); G. Feuerer, *Ordnung zum Ewigen* (Regensburg, 1934); U. Holzmeister, *Gaudete in Domino* (VD 22, 1942, 257–262); J. Brosch, *Jesus und die Freude* (M-Gladbach, 1946); *LThK,* 2nd ed., IV 361f (E. Schick, A. Auer). On the dialectic of joy and suffering: P. T. Dehau, *Joie et tristesse* (Paris, 1946); Jean Massin, "Le rire et la croix" in *Études Carmélitaines* [1947] 88–116; M. Carrez, "Souffrance et gloire dans les épîtres pauliniennes" in *RHPh* 31 (1951) 343–353); A. Brunner, "Das Geheimnis der christlichen Freude" in *Geist und Leben* (1953): 414–422); W. Nauck, "Freude im Leiden" in *ZNW* 46 (1955): 68–80.

(Aristotle): in ethicizing man's whole subethical realm. The more exalted a view of man is taken by ethics or religion, the nearer they place him to God and the eternal, the more renunciation they will demand of him, either in the form of asceticism (India), the martyr's courage (Socrates) or the pitiless imperative that requires all egoistic criteria to be subordinated to universally human and social demands (Kant). In the face of death, a Christian like Boethius can quite rightly draw consolation from philosophy.

The individual and the social points of view go hand in hand. Nietzsche can demand that the individual undergo every pain, every imaginable self-conquest in the interest of self-cultivation, since a "great" man only becomes such in countering opposition. *Ho mē dareis anthropos ou paideuetai:* spare the rod and spoil the child. And the way out of the Kantian "either/or" between inclination and absolute duty is by no means to be found in a compromise between the two (nor did Schiller ever mean to suggest that it was), but either in the inclinations being assimilated to duty (which calls for continual sacrifice), or in discovering an attraction in duty itself. This can happen in two ways: either by developing in oneself a greater inclination for the general good than for the private good (Hegel, Marx), or where the "categorical imperative" itself inclines toward man as categorically selfless love (as in Christianity).

Let us dwell for a moment on the first possibility. Hegelian philosophy develops such a passion for truth's completeness ("absolute knowledge") that it blithely sacrifices not only the individual's happiness but also his human and eternal existence for the sake of this "highest good". From philosophers, at least, it demands that this sacrifice be deliberate. It is a "speculative Good Friday" (although Hegel understands this somewhat differently from the way we do here), in which the individual surrenders everything that is distinctive of him in order to be subsumed into the integration of the Whole—which will appropriate him in any case. But whereas the compulsory expropriation of all that is private for the sake of the common good is characterized by pain and death, its philosophical accompaniment has the quality of an ultimate liberation, satisfaction and joy. And in Marx' variation this implies the following: as a dialectical historical process the expropriation of private property in favor of common ownership has a ruthless and indeed catastrophic face, but the conscious side of it is that, by understanding and affirming the process, one is sacrificing one's personal happiness for the happiness of (future) mankind. And here lies the insoluble paradox of Marxism: the *joy* of self-surrender for this eschatological ideal (which I personally shall not live to enjoy) is actually greater than the envisioned *happiness* of a humanity that will no longer have any need to go beyond itself in such a heroic manner. In the same way, for Hegel, "absolute knowledge" was of less moment than the joy of collaborating, through self-sacrifice, in its discovery. For modern man (as in Homer, the tragic tradition and Aristotle) it is man, struggling and suffering man, who is more significant than God the spectator; painful yearning for the Absolute is more significant than the painless, self-enclosed "knowledge of knowledge".

The difference is that in modern times there is also an awareness of the process itself (evolution). No doubt that is why every day we calmly accept reports of ever-intensifying war and famine, and the threat of total destruction of mankind at all levels, as the inevitable public sacrifice that must be offered to a transcendent ideal that increasingly disappears into the mist. At least, that is the only possible excuse for it. Once we realize, however, that in practical terms this ideal is unattainable, it is a fact that the genuine sacrificial joy that could have sustained us during the early stages fades away. It becomes clear, from the secular stand-point, that the path on which we have set out (and there is no other) cannot be followed to its completion.

A miracle needs to take place: the most unyielding categorical imperative of self-transcendence must coincide with the most blissful inclination of love. And this is only possible in Christianity, where God is not "thought thinking itself" and "absolute knowledge" but triune love—a love that comes to us from its origin in the shape of the incarnate Son, taking upon himself, on his Cross, our ultimate failure and hence our loss of joy, and in himself transforming our attempts to go beyond ourselves into new joy through a "hope that does not deceive".

3

The first biblical steps run parallel to those of individual and social ethics, but infuse a new soul into them in anticipation of the end in view. Thus the father's stern

chastisement of the child, which is an educative blessing springing from love (Prov 13:24),[10] follows the
example of God's loving and educative chastisement of
Israel (Dt 8:5f.; Prov 3:11f.)—an idea that is made
much of by the Letter to the Hebrews (Heb 12:5–13)
and that Paul applies to his own chastising role in the
community (1 Cor 11:21–32), a role that is already the
sign of the eschatological kindness of the God who
exercises judgment (cf. 1 Pet 4:17; Rev 3:19). This
presupposes that the meaning and purpose of the process are not evident to the child but to the father, that
is, God; for the present, the child only experiences
sorrow, pain and tears. Only in faith and as a result of
admonition in faith can Christians understand that
such treatment shows them to be sons: "For the moment all discipline seems painful rather than pleasant;
later it yields the peaceful fruit of righteousness to
those who have been trained by it" (Heb 12:11). This
"seems" *(dokein)* is repeated in the apostle's chastisement
of the community. The Christian dialectic is to be
found at a deeper level: his letter grieved the Corinthians, "though only for a while", and this grief was a
proper, "godly" grief. Insofar as it was "godly" (not
insofar as it was "grief"!) it occasioned the apostle joy
(2 Cor 7:8–9), and now he expects the community,
having understood the joy that lies in his role of admonishment, to share it: "I felt sure of all of you, that
my joy would be the joy of you all" (2 Cor 2:3). But
this joy can only be reached through the proper sorrow
of the one under correction: "For if I cause you pain,

[10] Prov 22:15; 23:13, 14; 29:15–17; Job 5:17; Sir 30:1, 8, 12.

who is there to make me glad but the one whom I have pained?" (2 Cor 2:2). This taking the risk of paining someone in order to harvest (and subsequently sow) joy far exceeds the logic of the Old Testament: it is a thoroughly christological logic of the Cross. It is a reflection of the attitude of Christ, who brings his followers with him to the Cross and expects them to understand it as an "education" ("I am the Way") for joy, motivated by joy and leading back to it.

However, it is part of this educative process and this way that an estrangement occurs at the moment when this joy is withdrawn. And whoever is accompanying the disciple—the Lord or his apostle—must make it clear that this estrangement is something unavoidable and normal. "Beloved, do not be surprised at the fiery ordeal which comes upon you to prove you, as though something strange were happening to you. But rejoice insofar as you share Christ's sufferings" (1 Pet 4:12f.). "Count it all joy, my brethren, when you meet various trials" (James 1:2). This first passage asserts that the motivation for going through the "fire" is that of sharing Christ's sufferings, which will enable those who do so to share his glory in joy and jubilation (at the *parousia*); but it goes on to point to that attitude in suffering that—inwardly assimilating the attitude of Christ—provides the transition from endurance to joy: "Therefore let those who suffer according to God's will do right and entrust their souls to a faithful Creator" (1 Pet 4:19). The passage from James indicates the same transition, by referring to the "testing of your faith" in suffering, which produces steadfastness that in turn leads to the *eschaton* (cf. Mt 10:22, 24:13). Paul even rejoices "in our sufferings, knowing that suffering produces endurance, and endurance produces character, and character produces hope, and hope does not disappoint us, because God's love has been poured into our hearts through the Holy Spirit which has been given to us" (Rom 5:3–5). In Paul, "rejoice", "glory", "boast" often mean the same thing: it is something he can do even when afflicted, because the chain of inner dispositions he describes not only reaches to the "hope of glory" (v. 2) but actually renders this glory present in the Spirit. Thus, "though now for a little while you may have to suffer various trials", it is for two purposes: to test the genuineness of faith and to purify it (and make it more genuine). This is already a cause for "rejoicing" in anticipation[11] "with unutterable and exalted joy" (1 Pet 1:6–8). In all these related trains of thought it is precisely the alienating aspect of suffering that is the pledge, and even the hidden presence, of eschatological joy. It is this hidden presence that enables Paul to qualify even the most acute suffering—insofar as it is a suffering with Christ—as *"quasi"*: *quasi tristes, semper autem gaudentes* (2 Cor 6:10; cf. Heb 12:11: *videtur non esse gaudii*). For all pain and grief belong essentially to the dimension of time, which, measured against the "eternal weight of glory", is a "slight, momentary affliction" (2 Cor 4:17).

However, "testing" and "purifying" are insufficient to constitute what is specifically Christian; they exist

[11] Since *angalliasthe* in verse 8 refers to the faith which does not see, the same word in verse 6 should also be understood in a present, not a future sense [as, e.g., Luther's German Bible—Tr.].

already in the Old Covenant.[12] If grief and trials are to be Christian and a participation in Christ, they themselves must be destined to be handed on to others. Experience of suffering cannot be evaluated privately but only within the communion of saints, both in terms of making Christian suffering available for others and of imparting a soothing consolation to them in their suffering. For Paul "shares abundantly in Christ's sufferings", and it is this that simultaneously promotes both pain and consolation in him (2 Cor 1:4–7). This is a law, and as such cannot be limited to the apostle in his mediating relationship between Christ and the community: it must be the expression of a general principle that continues to apply in post-apostolic times insofar as all participation in the Lord's suffering is designed to be passed on. And just as suffering and consolation are inextricably intertwined in the believer who has a share in Christ, it is essential that what is imparted to the Church and the world shall not be a one-sided "consolation" (for example, in the sense of sparing it suffering) but also a handing on of participation in suffering in the Church, "for the sake of his body, that is, the Church" (Col 1:24). At this point, we must refer to the most magnificent example of this dialectic in the early Church, namely, Ignatius of Antioch. Pursuing his painful path to martyrdom, he not only overflowed himself with the consolation of Christ, he also strengthened the churches by carrying them with him into his sharing of Christ's suffering and consolation.

[12] Gen 22:1; Prov 17:3; 27:21; Jer 11:20f; Mal 3:3.

Nor is this all. Suffering that is consoled is not ultimate suffering, it is not the Cross. Our topic is not "joy and suffering" but "joy and the Cross". It is not Paul, but John, who lifts the last veil here. Paul always thinks of the Cross from the standpoint of the Resurrection, in accordance with his vision on the Damascus road. But John accompanies his Master along his path into suffering. Paul can rejoice at the accomplished fact that "the love of Christ"[13] has demonstrated itself in the ultimate surrender, in becoming sin and a curse. John's love must have caused him to assent from the outset to this terrible decision on the part of his Master and friend. John's deepest, most excruciating suffering ultimately consists in the fact that he must let him suffer without making any objection, without being able to call a halt. The dark shadow of the Cross falls over Jn 12–17 right from the start: just as Jesus himself is "troubled" (13:21; cf. 11:33, 12:27), he speaks to those who are "troubled" with him (14:1); a troubled Jesus consoles those who are likewise troubled by pointing out, as Paul does, that the suffering will only last a "little while" (16:16)—though for him, genuinely forsaken by God, it will be a suffering that is timeless. He compares this "little while" to a woman's pains in childbirth, in which the joy of before and after are submerged under the pain of the now. Here, therefore, there is no longer any talk of a Pauline *"quasi"*, in fact, things are completely reversed: "Truly, truly, I say to you, you will weep and lament, but the world will

13 Rom 8:35, 37; 2 Cor 5:14; Gal 2:20; Eph 3:19; 5:2, 25. This love on the part of Christ manifests the love of God the Father: Rom 5:8; 8:39.

rejoice." And only then comes the change: "but your sorrow will turn into joy", that is, it will be in the past, just as a woman forgets her fear once the child arrives. With the prospect of the Cross before him, casting its shadow in advance, Jesus—almost unbelievably—demands that his loving disciples embrace his coming Passion with joy: "If you loved me, you would have rejoiced, because I go to the Father" (14:28), that is, via the path chosen by the Father, which leads through the Cross.[14]

That is why John brings together the three (female) representatives of the loving Church in the events of the Passion and Resurrection: Mary of Bethany, who lovingly anoints the Lord for his burial (that is, anoints him as the suffering Messiah); Mary the Mother, who has to perfect her consent under the Cross, including her being sent away to a new son; and Mary Magdalen, who, on Easter morning, has to consent to the Son's returning to the Father and accept that she cannot hold him—and she is sent to his brethren instead. The demands made on the man Jesus by the Cross, the drama of the world's sin, are simply excessive; the demand made of the loving Church is no less excessive, in that it is required to consent to this nameless suffering on the part of its Beloved. Even more excessive is the fact that the loving Church is expected to affirm—with rejoicing! (Jn 14:28)—that Jesus' entire soul (and not merely the "lower parts of the soul") was forsaken by God and that he descended into hell (and not merely into some antechamber of hell that was still illumi-

[14] On what follows cf. the author's "Ist die Messe ein Opfer der Kirche?" in *Spiritus Creator* (1967), 166–217.

nated by faith, love and hope!)—and that it is expected to accompany him thither.

Now, in the "Church between the times", the paradox between Cross and joy reaches its full dimensions, because the Church can never see the Cross as something that lies behind it as an accomplished fact in past historical time, any more than it can regard its sinfulness as a closed issue in the past. It can never establish itself so completely in the Easter event—and hence in Easter joy—that it no longer needs to be continually accompanying Jesus on the way to the Cross. For the Church is not only the sinner who rejoices that she will soon be freed from her sins but also the lover who sees clearly what a price the Beloved will have to pay for this redemption. Has Protestantism given sufficient reflection to this?

It is due to this strange paradox that Christian joy has a uniquely burning and consuming quality. When Paul is writing words of consolation to his suffering fellow Christians he can encourage them in terms of a pure and peaceful joy—just as Jesus speaks a pure, peaceful joy to his disciples in his farewell discourses—but as far as his own personal joy is concerned, a gale is always blowing through it, constantly fanning the flames: "For the love of Christ has totally seized possession of us[15], because we are convinced [after ade-

---

[15] *Sunechein* means more than simply "constraineth" (AV) or "controls" (RSV)—in view of the two poles given in the preceding verse, i.e., being "beside ourselves" and being "in our right mind"— it goes beyond both these states, thus: "totally takes possession of". The element of pressure, of spurring on, is also present here, rightly translated by the Vulgate's *caritas enim Christi urget nos*.

quate reflection: *krinantes,* since it is a case of making a *krina,* a decision] that one has died for all; therefore all have died" (2 Cor 5:14f.). In any case, it is a joy that can never settle down anywhere to enjoy worldly goods; even in genuine pleasure, it keeps its gaze on the love of Christ as it is expressed in the Church (cf. Phil 4:10–19; 1 Cor 10:31). We cannot do justice to New Testament theology by simply relating earthly goods (in our enjoyment of them) to eternal goods. Nor is it a case of a simple alternation of joy and suffering (for instance, according to the seasons of the Church's year), for everything is evaluated and ordered from a single eschatological standpoint. Nor can there be any question of relativizing the Cross as a result of Easter joy, for the Christian's discipleship can enter the dark night of the Spirit, not only mystically but in the many kinds of *desolatio,* as long as man is subject to the law of temporal existence. Nor can the Church's vantage point be simply described as essentially post-Easter and the Christian's cast of mind be deduced from it, undialectically. In fact, life in the Church remains in the unfathomable "between the times" mystery. Indeed, it lies deeper still: the Church's understanding of the relationship between Cross and joy is to be found in the realm of the mystery of Jesus' Cross: only in virtue of his filial intimacy with the divine Father can he suffer total abandonment by the Father and taste that suffering to the last drop.

6. The three forms of hope

I. On the history of hope

The bigger the catchword, the smaller the issue. People only begin to talk about culture when it has become ambivalent. Nowadays there is so much talk of hope because people are trying to cling to something that is hurrying away from them. It has always been clear that, while a purely this-worldly hope can provide man, hovering in uncertainty as he is, with a stimulus for action and even a reason for living, it can never guarantee fulfillment. If it is to be more than a blind urge, it must be able to find a firm foothold for the totality of this hovering existence. The history of hope in the West goes through four phases: the ancient, the biblical, the phase of Christian thought (in which the biblical view is supported by the best achievements of the ancient world) and the modern, in which this support drops away and man is faced with a decision of apocalyptic implications.

1. The ancient phase

Elpis signifies every human expectation, good or evil. While it is occasionally portrayed as indispensable to human life, the momentum it generates is praised (Pindar, Isthm. 8:15: "Man must hope for the good") and its consoling power is recognized (Thucydides, V 103), yet for the most part we are warned against its seductive power, the fact that it cuts both ways (Theognis, 637f.). Basically, man can only depend on his *promatheia,* his reflection on the present that grants him a little foresight as to what is coming: an initial, elementary futurology (Pindar, Nem. 11:46). "Chance is generous but unreliable, whereas nature rests in itself, which is why, with its lesser but dependable [power], it vanquishes the greater [promise] of hope" (Democritus, Fragm. 176). This is because the relationship between the gods and men is upset. It has become a relationship of cunning and compulsion that is expressed by that between the "reflecting" Prometheus and Zeus. Prometheus deceives Zeus in sacrifice, ensuring that he gets the worst pieces; in recompense, Zeus conceals the goods man needs in order to live so that he has to struggle for them in the sweat of his brow (Hesiod, Erg. 42ff.). Now Prometheus steals fire in order to give "blind hope" back to men (Aeschylus, Prom. 5:20). As a punishment, Zeus sends Pandora with her box. According to one version, the box contains all good things, but must not be opened. However, man does open it, the good things fly back to the gods and, when the lid is snapped shut, all that remains on earth is hope (Babrius, 58). In the other version, the temptress (Pan-dora, the "all-giving") releases all evils from the box; the only thing left in the box is hope (Hesiod, Erg. 94ff.). But the dawn of Western culture already points to its end. The strongest theme of the legend is that in the beginning Prometheus[1] created men from clay and looks after his race—implying that mankind has a Promethean self-sufficiency—whereas Zeus replies by creating woman, which shatters human self-sufficiency and replaces it with hope, present yet unattainable and at the very least problematical. In the end, Western culture will have seriously to confront the issue of man's Promethean self-creation versus his dependence on Zeus; it will also have to face hope's helpless aspiration above and beyond earthly "reflection" to some event that will take place between heaven and earth.

Philosophy attempts to anchor this vacillating hope in a "beyond" that is—from an earthly point of view—utopian. There seems to be a dim awareness of something in Heraclitus' strange fragment: "Unless he hopes for it he will not find the unhoped for, since it cannot be tracked down and is inaccessible" (Fragm. 18). Does he mean that which lies beyond all that can be hoped for? Or does he attain it by the power of his own hoping? In Plato, too, there are religious prospects of immortality behind his "hopefulness" (Apol. 41c; Phaed. 64a), as also in Aristophanes, when, in the face of the duality of the sexes, which were originally one, and of that unity that starts up again in the earthly

---

[1] On the origins and various forms of the Prometheus myth cf. the essays by W. Aly, A. Rolet, K. von Fritz, F. Wehrli, E. Heitsch collected by E. Heitsch in *Hesiod* (*Wege der Forschung* XLIV, 1966).

enjoyment of love, he embraces the "future of the greatest hopes" (Symp. 193d). But the twilight that, in Plato, continues to envelop the personality or impersonality of the world's artificer has an effect on the destiny of the idea of personal immortality: in the Stoa and in large tracts of Neoplatonism the all-pervading divine principle of reason becomes impersonal, and wisdom has to be assimilated to it, involving the surrender of the will for personal immortality. Resignation, not hope, has the last word here: "Leave off vain hopes" (Marcus Aurelius, 3:14). A static "providence", identical with itself, embraces the universe, that is, material, animal and human nature—one must submit to it for it is always in the right.

2. The Bible

Everything changes when the Promethean suspicion of God, the uncertainty about his (and hence my) personality, disappears, because Israel's whole existence rests on the prevenient saving activity of God, who is both free and personal. Hope, founded on God's great deeds in history and on his unchangeable and explicitly promised faithfulness, is totally positive as it awaits good things from him. It is identical with trust in God. But God's actions cannot be controlled, and this means that *prometheia* is of no avail where he is concerned: the only appropriate response is that of patient waiting and taking refuge in him (Ps 4:6, 12:6, 26:12, 32:18, 22, 36:3 etc.). And yet this hope too remains paradoxical, dialectical—in the first place because the Covenant is bilateral, requiring a particular attitude on man's part as one of the conditions, namely, genuine faith (even when God seems to fail to respond), the keeping of the commandments and the implementation, so far as it lies in man's power, of righteousness on earth toward his fellowman. In earlier times, bloody wars were also part of obedience to God, and so eventually the question will arise as to how far political self-liberation can make, as it were, an active contribution to "waiting in hope". In Judaism, after the advent of Christianity, the grave question arises as to whether the approach of the Messianic age may or should be "speeded up", by more fervent prayer or perhaps by political action.

There is a further paradox: classical Israel hopes for an earthly future and does not expect personal immortality (Is 38:18; Job 17:15; Ezek 37:11 etc.). And even when this hope, which initially looks for God's immediate intervention, gradually turns in a more and more eschatological direction, its prime goal is a "resurrection of the nation", not of the individual. The idea of personal immortality only gains ground quite late, under the influence of other religions. Israel opens up the realm of a saving future for mankind in a generic sense. And since the Covenant is bilateral, the dominant hope is always sharply qualified by the idea of judgment: God will judge not only the enemy, but faithless Israel as well. But the sense of powerlessness under God's judgment becomes a stimulus to new hope.

The fact of Christ's Resurrection breaks through this structure of hope from all sides. The expectation of a generic resurrection is intercepted by the fact that mortals living in the old aeon actually encounter a single individual who has risen from the dead in eschatological time. Thus eschatological reality cuts across the world's time: on the one hand, the expectation of the future is fanned to white heat (in the primitive Church's expectation of the immediate *parousia,* in the longing for death and the life beyond on the part of martyrs and later Christians); on the other hand, it is dampened, for in Christ the heavenly city has been conquered. Compared with this, what relevance has any hope in an earthly future? Moreover, the Lord has risen as a person; consequently, each individual can hope for salvation and fear judgment. Thus hope becomes necessarily individual and the connection between personal and social hope is harder to grasp.

But if, in Christian terms, hope still hovers and cannot be tied down—"Now hope that is seen is not hope" (Rom 8:24)—the "hope of being freed" (8:21) rests not only on faith in the Resurrection of the "first fruits", which has already taken place; rather, it is a hope in which, with "the Spirit interceding for us with sighs" (1:26), we possess the "guarantee" (Eph 1:14; lit. "deposit") of total salvation "laid up" in God. Thus God is a "God of hope" (Rom 15:13), both as its goal and in accompanying the act of hope. As a result, even temptation and the apparent obscuring of and obstacles to hope can contribute to strengthening and establishing it (5:3–5) and to deepening the "rejoicing in hope" (12:12). However, the clear transcendence of the Resurrection pushes the idea of hastening the approach of the Messianic age right into the background: what remains to be done on earth is effectively to proclaim salvation in a way that embraces both words and deeds. Whereas the Jewish hope arises from unfulfillment and presses toward the dawning fulfillment, the Christian hope springs from the fulfillment attained in Christ and is shot through with the painful lack of fulfillment in man and the world.

3. The Christian era

Thus we have three models of hope: the pagan, the Jewish and the Christian. These three strive together for the meaning of life. In the Christian era, which lasts until modern times, the Jewish hope was enclosed in a ghetto, whereas the Christian hope entered a kind of alliance with that of the ancient world. Today this alliance has gone. Its extrabiblical form is still there but has become ultimately inert, whereas the Old and New Testament forms of hope offer each other stiff, dangerous and fruitful competition.

Even after the primitive Christian expectation of the Lord's imminent return had been overcome, the Christian era is still animated and sustained by the New Testament hope, now open to the world and going beyond itself to a new heaven and a new earth. The hidden presence of eschatological realities means that this "going beyond" seems less like a historical forward movement and more like a continual arrival, wave on wave, on the shore of eternity. However, the whole world, in its need of redemption, is kept intact by a good providence after the manner of Platonism or Stoicism: this underpins the cosmos as a whole, of which man and history form a part. And if the personal element of Christianity—each person must appear before God's judgment seat (2 Cor 5:10)—often casts dark shadows across the picture of the world, rendered even more somber by a wrathful doctrine of predestination (from the later Augustine via Gottschalk to Calvin and Jansen), Christendom was always on guard against a Gnostic-Manichaean dichotomy in the world. In its totality, the world is the wholesome and healed world of a loving God who cares for everything that exists. Hope remains poised and hovering in a form of certainty that is "hard to describe" and that it shares with faith, without being *perversa securitas* (Augustine);[2] taken as a whole, this hope comes through intact, supported by the awareness of an all-embracing cosmic order.

At the end of modern times, this peaceful poise becomes unsettled; arising from the Reformation new shadows are cast over the soul's landscape, to be fought off by a nervous "certainty of salvation". Then rationalism and the Enlightenment introduce a glaring light that threatens the "gift of fear" and favors a particular sentiment, namely, that "everything will work out for the best". This sentiment is heightened to the limit in the speculations of German Idealism on the World Spirit, which evolves into the Absolute Spirit in an ascending series of life forms through nature and history—a view that seems to receive unexpected confirmation from the theory of biological evolution. Now life's thrust toward self-transcendence and ever more perfect reflection no longer needs the religious

[2] J. Pieper, "Hoffnung" in *Handbuch theologischer Grundbegriffe I* (1962) 704; idem, *Über die Hoffnung* (1935) (English translation: *On Hope,* San Francisco: Ignatius, 1986]).

hope, which is replaced by knowledge or perhaps even by predictability.

4. The modern crisis

German Idealism abrogates the pact between Christianity and the thought of the ancient world. Its starting point is the absolute presence of the "I" to itself (Fichte), the element of absoluteness found in human freedom (Schelling) and the conviction that spirit can conceive the totality of the real (Hegel). This approach puts a question mark over the idea that what is absolute in man's spirit owes its existence to some other category, that is, God. True, insofar as man is the term of a long chain of ascending natural forms, he is determined by them, but once having attained the absolute standpoint of his free "I", he is empowered to recapitulate, through thought, the preconditions of his own existence. Thus he can understand them as conditions he himself has laid down, and in the same breath he can go on to take providential charge of his own history, which will consist essentially in coming to grips with and assimilating (humanizing) these preconditions of his. The entire medieval ontology of natural forms *(essentiae)* participating in a limited way in the infinite act of reality *(esse)* is here transformed into a part of anthropology: man acknowledges these forms to be preliminary stages of his own self, conditions of his own possibility. Physics, chemistry, biology, physiology, genetics and heredity, depth psychology with its urges and archetypes and so on are the infrastructure of his existence, which he increasingly recognizes and hence is increasingly able to manipulate by various techniques and technologies: the transition from Hegel's total theory to Marx's total practice of man's self-creation, by the penetration and control of nature in terms of "labor", is now inevitable. "World history" is now "nothing other than the creation of man through human labor"; "thus he has irrefutable proof as to who gave him birth: he himself" (Marx).[3] It is the ideal of total cybernetics, which seems to have come round once more to the ancient, Promethean attitude toward reality. Hegel's cunning on the part of reason becomes, in Marxist dress, man's: through the cunning of his labor he gets back the spark (which belongs to him as his own) that had been alienated from him.

To the extent that this process is successful and its success demonstrates it to be true and inevitable, man and the world are joined seamlessly together; even "atheism", seen as the denial of a human prospect of a "beyond", is "no longer meaningful",[4] nor is the opposition between "spiritualism and materialism"[5] Naturally this means that the category of "providence", in the sense of the ancient world and of Christianity, simply disappears, together with the existential attitude it informs. There is no place for prayer or hope where the whole responsibility for man's success, his history and future, rests on human "pro-vidence" (fore-sight, *prometheia*), cleverness and skill. But the

---

[3] "Nationalökonomie und Philosophie" in *Frühschriften,* ed. S. Landshut (1953), 247f., cf. 269: "man's self-creation . . . through his own work".

[4] Ibid., 248.

[5] Ibid., 243.

very moment this *prometheia* moves from the realm of thought (Hegel) to the sphere of action, the Old Testament *pathos* once more makes its appearance with compelling force—in the radical form of a "hastening" of the Messianic kingdom, not for the individual but for the people and society. For Marx, it is only the man who has identified himself with society who is a genuine human being.[6]

II. The three world views still possible today

Let us examine the world views that are still possible today, not in the abstract, but in the context of the actually existing theoretical and practical interrelationship of man and nature. This circle in which the serpent bites its tail, that is, man as conditioned, man who endeavors to gain control, through labor, of the conditions of his existence, is a reality. Indeed, it is not only one reality among others: it is a determinant pattern. What is our attitude toward it?

1. The Asiatic way out

For nonbiblical man, *elpis* was always embivalent; Prometheus, for exercising cunning in his dealings with Zeus, was fixed for aeons to the Caucasian rock. For Parmenides, Plato and Plotinus, the only way out of the vicious circle of the world's appearances was in philosophy's perpendicular, vertical ascent. Even after

[6] Ibid., 236ff.

the demise of Platonism, the Far East has continued to put forward this solution, in Brahmanism and Buddhism, as a meaningful path; indeed it is more meaningful than ever now that the vicious circle of *"sansara"*, the senselessly turning wheel of fallen existence, has adopted the acute Idealistic-Marxist form of man's self-creation. Is not society's whole labor process the eternally recurrent cycle of need and the satisfaction of need, that is, that demonic "thirst" *(tṛṣṇa)* from which Buddha bade us flee? And after Goethe, Western pagan thought has nothing better to offer than the despairing Nietzschean dialectic between the Promethean "Onward!" (toward the Superman) and being obliged to affirm the wheel's turning ("eternal recurrence"). This contradiction can only be overcome by distance—indeed, evasion. Freedom only exists in leaping out of the circle, in the negation of being subject to "needs", in the negation of differences as being merely superficial and illusory. Schopenhauer, along with Hegel and Marx, was the third huge influence in the area of *Weltanschauung* in the nineteenth century. Nowadays, technology itself is obliged to render its tribute to the path of evasion: the state of spiritual absorption attainable through great psychological effort can now be obtained cheaply through the use of drugs (which originated in the East and infiltrated the intelligentsia of Europe in the nineteenth century). People seriously discuss the equivalence of Buddhist-Eckhartian mysticism with that induced by drugs, and even the possibility of manipulating it (a self-sustained and controlled ecstasy)—in open defiance of the Marxist labor *ethos*. A similar attitude can be seen in the antitechnological movement among young people who scornfully ignore the offers of the consumer society. It has long been recognized that this kind of schizophrenia on the part of two societies living side by side is bound to render the globe uninhabitable. Ultimately, the antitechnological group will have to join forces with the explosive forces inherent in technology, and the rebellion against the compulsory socializing of the individual will turn into anarchy.

2. The Jewish utopian breakthrough

If evasion is impossible and a betrayal of man's commission to appropriate the world, this tragic law that man can only come to himself through realizing himself in nature (and can never bring this self-realization to an end) must be pierced by a prophetic ray of hope, namely, that the closed circle of man and world—the Messianic breakthrough into the realm of freedom— will succeed in spite of everything. In Marx, the Old Testament dualism between law (a slave morality externally imposed upon me by a master God) and prophesy, which bursts through this alienation in advance and promises an identity between the spontaneity of the heart and the "fulfillment of the law" (Jer 31:33)—the dualism with which Kafka torments himself—is to be overcome. Marx prefaces all tragic history by describing man in terms of "naturalism and humanism"[7] and projecting this definition, as a (Mes-

[7] Loc. cit., 275.

sianic) ideal, into the future, where it will realize itself through the historical processes it will have to undergo. Using the model of the Hegelian absolute *knowledge* (which is a closed circle),[8] Marx reads off the inevitable success of the absolute *action* he envisages. In order to arrive at that perfect freedom, in which the reciprocal realization of man and nature must bring fulfillment (love), all the severities of the historical dialectic are accepted. The call for a philosophy without presuppositions will lead to an (initially unintended) materialism; knowledge (not hope!) of the goal to be attained will lead to economic determinism; the ever-increasing manipulation and technologizing of human labor will in the first instance actually lead further away from its hoped-for humanization (as the Frankfurt workers had to discover, to their horror); the need to implement the prophesy demands that the totality that is being aimed for should appear as the Party. All these provisional elements harden and retard the leap into the realm of freedom, just as the advent of the Messiah was delayed in the case of Israel. Consequently, the ideal that is expected to emerge within the circle as "positive humanism" acquires a more and more patently utopian character: its reality lies ever more clearly in the "hope against all hope" of the prophet, for whom the "hope principle" is absolutely fundamental (E. Bloch). The dichotomy between law and prophesy takes many forms: there is the elemental "urge" (Scheler), which has the weight of reality to

[8] Marx shows its Promethean character in his doctoral dissertation. Loc. cit., 14.

overpower all ideal constructs; the primal instinctual energy (Freud), which scrutinizes and criticizes its own censorship laws; the vital energy, which crystallizes into forms only to burst them again (Bergson, Simmel); and finally, the power of the race, which presses forward to embrace a particular territory (Zionism) and yet, in its basic form, wishes to be not an isolated nation but the model of the true, open human being as such (from Mendelssohn via Marx, who did not want to be a Jew, to Rosenzweig and Buber). But however the dichotomy between law and prophesy is viewed, between alienation and the overcoming of it, between the particular nation and the promise addressed to the whole of mankind (the dichotomy that Hegel—following Luther—had identified as the tragic essence of Israel), it all goes to prove the correctness of the diagnosis of J. Taubes: "Israel is the restless element in world history, the leaven which alone actually creates history".[9] In virtue of its prophetic essence, Israel has taken philosophical Idealism and scientific evolutionism and made them into a pragmatism that presses forward relentlessly. It has done this by unmasking Hegelianism as the ultimate decadent form of a Christianity that showed itself incapable of changing the world and carrying out man's mandate in and to the world. It wrests Christianity's principle of "love of neighbor" from it, to apply it in earnest, showing compassion for the outcast and venting its wrath upon the oppressors. But how can it introduce salvation—

[9] *Abendländische Eschatologie* (Berne, 1947), 15.

final, decisive salvation—into the vicious circle of man's self-manipulation?

3. The irruption of salvation in Christ

In Buddhism and Neojudaism it is man who liberates himself. That is why they so often exhibit similarities: in Gnosticism and the Kabbalah, which assume that man's genuine core of freedom is trapped in matter, and that it is necessary to free him from it—thus G. Scholem, H. Jonas, the paintings of Chagall, not forgetting Schoenberg's Moses and Aaron. Nor should one forget all that remains unsaid and ineffable in Wittgenstein, the images of the Kingdom that are so magically evoked, perpendicular to horizontal history, in Karl Lowith and even more in Walter Benjamin. Nor, finally, should one forget that when, after Auschwitz, the German voice fell silent, fragments of Yahweh's genuine speech were put into the mouth of a Paul Celan and a Nelly Sachs; furthermore, even the titanic efforts of the structuralists (Levi-Strauss) to capture all reality within the web of the self-positing Word have a biblical origin: In the beginning was the Word, through which everything was created. Such cross-relationships do exist. And this only shows all the more clearly how profoundly Christianity today is challenged by the one partner that needs to be taken seriously. Anti-Semitism can no longer harm it. The challenge must be accepted and responded to honorably.

As far as Christianity is concerned two things are

clear: a faith that is based on the Incarnation cannot have recourse to flight from the world, and a faith that comes wholly from God's initiative is prohibited from "hastening" salvation by its own efforts. Initially this is confusing: the prohibition of a flight from the world seems to direct attention to a temporal future, whereas the prohibition against our building the Kingdom of God in the future seems to direct our gaze to a "beyond", suggesting flight from the world. The Christian has to take up man's task in the world without succumbing to the Promethean temptation; moreover, he must work together for the salvation of man and the world, knowing that the task cannot be completed within an earthly context. As a result of today's situation, he also knows that man, placed in history to exercise his freedom, can no longer count on a (Stoic) providence embracing him in the form of nature, guiding the destiny of nations in such a way as to prevent the explosion of atomic bombs, for instance. He himself must look after such things. It is as if "providence" has retreated a step higher or lower: it is a providence in Jesus Christ, who has enveloped the world and world history with his Cross-and-Resurrection event. *That* is now ultimate. But it is the most real event possible; its power, understood in New Testament terms, is always present. Sharing in it by faith, hope and love, the Christian carries out his task of shaping the world, not only according to his needs and abilities, but according to God's salvation. He does this by a power that transcends his own natural powers, and by a hope that is "against [the] hope" (Rom 4:18) of this aeon, because it arises from the Resurrection from the dead and from eternal life, contrary to the earthly hope, which is undermined by the death of each individual and by the "vanity" of the whole. Here the Christian hope is clearly distinct from the Jewish: rather than applying prophetic, Promethean force to change the alienating "law", that is, the structure of existence and society, it wants, as far as temporal conditions will allow, to fill this structure with the spontaneity of Christian love that God's Holy Spirit pours into our hearts (Rom 5:5). Even today, in the age of anthropology, man owes a debt of gratitude for what is most his own, even if he is never aware of his creaturely origin in God, and even less of the fact that he is "born of God" (Jn 1:13) by grace. It is not something he can manipulate with his technology. He is also indebted for his freedom, with its spark of absoluteness, which comes to him as a gift from eternal freedom. This mystery, this risk of endowing the creature with freedom is only possible within a view of God in which God gives himself absolute freedom (in the trinity of his life as Spirit). Thus the creature endowed with freedom is not overpowered and violated when God himself voluntarily accompanies it into the ultimate powerlessness of sin and isolation.

It is true that, seen in Christian terms, the world cannot be perfected at the natural level. Man, who is obliged to prove himself by engaging with the world and who grows through struggle, must achieve his full stature in failure. As Christian tradition—as represented by its best minds—has always known, man, with his world, is oriented beyond himself and toward God from the very outset, and not merely subsequently through being "raised to the state of grace". At this point Plato's and Buddha's intuitions were accurate. Henri de Lubac has shown this irrefutably in his great work on "the freedom of grace".[10] Ultimately, therefore, man fashions not only himself as an individual, but his social world too, in a way that goes beyond the world in the direction of God. He must plan as well as he can, but he cannot bring the fulfillment of his plan: there will never be enough room for the Kingdom of God in the straitened conditions of time. In spite of this, he cannot leave the responsibility for the Kingdom exclusively to God. He must responsibly employ the freedom he has gratefully received; he must double the talents entrusted to him.

Man's mystery is that he can pour the Spirit of the Eternal into the earthly vessels by way of anticipation—not by smashing or stretching them by prophetic, anarchistic violence but by transforming the "alienated" law from within by the spontaneity of love, liberating and lifting it to a new plane. Here he finds himself locked in the closest struggle with his Jewish brother. He cannot allow him any pride of place in taking responsibility for the poor and humiliated and for the future of mankind. He must make sure that his anger with the oppressors and his compassion with the oppressed rings true here and now. And the Christian can draw strength from the here and now—he does not need to console people with the promise of tomorrow. By exhibiting the here-and-now power of

[10] Two vols: I. The legacy of Augustine, II. The human paradox. (German translation: Einsiedeln: Johannes Verlag, 1971.)

love, of conversion, of committed action, he is beginning to change the world *today*. Today he is giving
direction and motion to things—albeit this motion,
from an empirical point of view, is continually being
unmasked as circular. Both direction and movement
are mysterious; they cannot be measured statistically.
(And externally things only become more apocalyptic.) But this is precisely the mystery of Christian
hope: wherever it is genuinely alive, it creates a whirl-
pool opening up to the depths. So, participating in the
all-embracing Providence we have called the Christ
event, the Christian who loves, intercedes and suffers
on others' behalf can help to guide the course of the
world. In the Christian perspective, the Cross is the
height of action: it continues to act where all else is
vain.

Christian hope causes the pagan and the Jewish hope
to encounter each other at a point that is beyond both
of them. It vindicates them both at a point beyond
them, just as it itself is aware that it receives everything
it is, and its credentials, from "the beyond".

III. The unity of times

In Buddhism and Platonism, transcendence operates
unequivocally *backward* in time. Here the movement of
re-ligio "binds back" to the lost origin. All forms of this
transcendence are concerned with recalling the past.
The soul's truth is obscured, but religious man knows
that it can be dug out from under the rubbish of what
is worldly and of the senses. Without having learned

them, the slave Menon knows the principles of arithmetic. The guru can recall his previous existences, spiritually approaching the point at which individuation, his falling from the Absolute, occurred. The only palliative for the baneful dissipation of existence is recollection in oneself, the mysterious path inward, into the depths, into "being" *(Wesen)* which is always a "having been" *(Ge-Wesen)*.

Judaic transcendence is unequivocally oriented to the future. When Israel recalls the great deeds of Yahweh, it is not to conjure them up as past events but to impart a new impetus to flagging hope. The Messianic Kingdom is ahead—what is to come is the open fourth wall, allowing man, trapped in the law, to breathe. "Remember not the former things, nor consider the things of old. Behold, I am doing a new thing: now it springs forth, do you not perceive it? I will make a way in the wilderness and rivers in the desert" (Is 43:18f.). Every way back is blocked in the present suffering; the only hope is that God will turn Israel's destiny and at last fulfill his promises. And if this God were no longer alive, man himself would have to hasten into the future to organize the fulfillment.

All that remains for Christianity, therefore, is the *present*. And this is its great strength. From this standpoint, the other two paths are ultimately only escape routes. For both of them the present is untruth. Existence, as it is lived in fact, cannot be right. It is alienated from itself. At least it can see enough of the truth to realize that. And the beginning of wisdom is the denial of what now is. Only Christianity has the courage to affirm the present, because God has affirmed it.

He became a man like ourselves. He lived in our alienation and died in our God-forsakenness. He imparted the "fullness of grace and truth" (Jn 1:17) to our here and now. He filled our present with his presence. But since the divine presence embraces all "past" and all "future" in itself, he has opened up to us all the dimensions of time. The Word that became flesh is the "Word in the beginning"; in him we have been "chosen before the foundation of the world". It is also the "final word", in which everything in heaven and on earth shall be caught up together: Alpha and Omega.

Only in Christianity can the opposed world views be reconciled. Both of them, the *memoria* and the *spes,* are already embraced by the real presence of God in the Eucharist. We gather around the Lord's table to celebrate the memorial of his Passion, but we do so with a view to his coming (1 Cor 11:26). But when, in the Christian *memoria,* we enter through contemplation into God's great deeds for us, we do not submerge into a timeless realm before the creation of the world in a Buddhist or Platonist sense: we immerse ourselves in the grace of God, which has always been there for us since before all time, and which has embraced us more purposefully than we can ever conceive. So this grace also opens up an unimaginable future ahead of us. Since Paul has grasped that "Jesus Christ has made me his own", he can speak of "forgetting what lies behind and straining forward to what lies ahead" (Phil 3:12ff.). It is not possession, but a being possessed, that lends wings to Christian hope. It vibrates with the thought that the earth should reply to heaven in the way that heaven has addressed earth. It is not in his own strength that the Christian wants to change the earth, but with the power of grace of him who—transforming all things—committed his whole self for him.

Because the Christian does not have to depend on his own resources to find himself, but has been situated and found by God, he can lose himself neither in the past nor in the future. "All things are yours: the world or life or death or the present or the future, all are yours; and you are Christ's; and Christ is God's" (1 Cor 3:21f.).